How MY SAVIOR Leads ME

Terri M. Stellrecht

WESTBOW
PRESS
A DIVISION OF THOMAS NELSON

*Scripture taken from the Holy Bible, New International
Version®. Copyright © 1973, 1978, 1984, 2010 Biblica. Used
by permission of Zondervan. All rights reserved.*

WestBow Press books may be ordered through booksellers or by contacting:

*WestBow Press
A Division of Thomas Nelson
1663 Liberty Drive
Bloomington, IN 47403
www.westbowpress.com
1-(866) 928-1240*

*ISBN: 978-1-4497-2572-3 (sc)
ISBN: 978-1-4497-2573-0 (hc)
ISBN: 978-1-4497-2571-6 (e)*

Library of Congress Control Number: 2011915199

Printed in the United States of America

WestBow Press rev. date: 11/09/2011

How
MY SAVIOR
Leads ME

An attempt to bring Glory to God for what
He has chosen to do with our lives.

A legacy to leave to my children in the telling of it.

In loving memory of Trent Lee Stellrecht~

Our son, Trent Lee Stellrecht, was born on March 10, 1998. God granted us 12 years with this precious boy before He chose to bring him home to heaven through a skiing accident on February 18, 2011.

Trent was a child that lived his life fully, with somewhat reckless abandon. He found great joy in hunting, fishing, building, playing football, and sliding down mud hills. But ultimately, his joy was found in his King and Savior, Jesus Christ, who he confidently proclaimed.

Trent will be remembered with many tears of joy for his life lived by his parents Rob and Terri Stellrecht, siblings Alexis, Cole, Grace and Micah, his grandmother, many aunts, uncles, pancake-eating cousins, and friends. He is preceded in death by his grandfather, Donald Lee.

It is with great rejoicing that we release our son, Trent Lee Stellrecht, age 12, to our Heavenly Father. Dance before your King, my son.

TABLE OF CONTENTS

PART 1
The Story

PART 2
Grief and God

PART 3
The Blog Posts

Everybody dies, but not everybody lives.

On Friday, February 18, 2011, God did the unthinkable in our life: He chose to take our 12-year-old son, Trent Lee Stellrecht, home to heaven in a skiing accident.

It is only considered "the unthinkable" because our plans are not God's plans, and our ways are not God's ways.

Before Trent was born we had entrusted the Lord with his life and had asked Him, above all else, to bring salvation to our son. Our greatest desire was that he would be used in a mighty way for God's glory, and that God would let him dwell in heaven for eternity.

God answered our prayers that Friday in a mightier way than we could have imagined, and we have been rejoicing in His good works and His mercies ever since.

Trent was a boy who truly lived. From the very beginning he did what he loved and enjoyed to the full the gifts and skills that God had given him. In his short life he saw much of this world, traveling as far as India, the Bahamas, and Missouri where he explored his favorite destination on his golden birthday: Bass Pro Shop, as well as many family camping trips. God instilled a love of hunting and fishing in Trent, and a joy of the great outdoors. Since he was little all he wanted was to turn 12 to be able to go deer hunting. During his 12th year God allowed him to shoot two deer. Trent loved to cook, to pick on his siblings Alexis, Cole, Grace, and Micah, to protect his mother, to snuggle with his father, and to be with his friends, especially his best friends: Thomas and Samuel. He tried everything that interested him, even carving his own long bow and succeeding in taxidermy. In his short years he lived life to the fullest.

But as we are all destined to, Trent also died. On Friday, February 18, 2011, we said goodbye to our son as he left for a skiing trip with his friends, not knowing that he would never be coming back home. God says that He knows the number of our days, that He has created each one of them, and that He will do what He pleases (Psalm 115:3; Job 14:5).

God's standards to enter His kingdom are high: He expects perfection. Trent was not perfect, not even close. God graciously provided His perfect Son, Jesus Christ, as the atonement for our sinfulness and requires that we simply believe and acknowledge Him for it. God does the rest.

For most of his life Trent struggled with his own sinfulness before God. He knew that he was not right before God, and nothing he could do would ever make up for the sins he had committed to make him worthy to enter heaven. In the spring of 2010, God graciously chose to bring salvation to Trent through repentance and the saving grace of Christ Jesus. Trent's life was transformed and we enjoyed the young fruit in his life as we watched God work.

It was with great peace and much rejoicing, then, that we as his family have sent him off before us and accepted God's perfect plan for Trent's life. Our longing is that God would be glorified in what He has done to wake up many to the realization that we are not guaranteed any number of years in this world (Psalm 39:4-5).

On Friday morning we had our son; on Friday afternoon he was gone.

What we have asked so many people since the accident is: "What if it had been you? Where would you be right now?"

We diligently raised Trent up to know his sinful state and taught him what the Word of God says because we know the implications of denying Christ now, and God was gracious to answer our prayers and to save him. Scripture says that the gospel will go forth with much sorrow and heartache. Please let Trent's short life be a wake-up call to you. We are rejoicing in the sorrow because we know where our son is and that we will one day be with him again for eternity because of our own salvation.

God's mercies are new every day and His peace does surpass all understanding (Lamentations 3:22-23; Phillipians 4:6-7). God has been so gracious to us by blessing us first of all with His peace in His perfect plan. The family and friends who have surrounded us and have lifted us up in prayer are amazing and another testimony to God's goodness.

It is with great rejoicing that we release our son, Trent Lee Stellrecht, age 12, to our Heavenly Father. Dance before your King, my son.

Introduction

Who am I to write a book on grief? I am certainly not an expert, but rather I am a mother who was granted this gift of suffering from God to learn to trust Him and know Him in a way that I never would have without it. Would I have ever dreamt about, let alone asked for, an opportunity to share God's grace and the gospel with hundreds, even thousands of people, if I had known how much it would cost me? That it would cost me my own son?

In one sense, no, but in another sense, yes. All those prayers of "God's will be done, not my own" have yielded my heart to accept what God chose to do in our lives on February 18, 2011, as good and perfect. Every night that I prayed for Trent that God would save him and use him in a mighty way, that He would allow him to spend an eternity in heaven, and that our family would bring glory to His name were answered that day.

As I ponder it more and more, has not my Heavenly Father chosen to answer my prayers for the salvation of my son in a glorious way that is beyond my earthly comprehension? When I get to heaven and see things clearly, will I not praise my God and Savior all the more for His utmost wisdom in how He chose to glorify His name in our lives? As my Savior, Jesus Christ, leads me I will walk through this valley of the shadow of death because I know who is holding my hand as we walk it together (Psalm 23; Isaiah 41:13). He is the one who said that

He would never leave me or forsake me and will guide me on this path to all righteousness as I trust in Him (Deuteronomy 31:6; Proverbs 4:11-12). May God be glorified in all that He does in my life.

Part 1

The Story

Simply God

Chapter 1

Turn to me and be saved, all you ends of the earth;
for I am God and there is no other.

Isaiah 45:22

God. I can't remember a time in my life when I did not know that He existed.

Somehow, somewhere, long ago, whether in some Sunday school classroom or playing out in the woods as a young girl, God was always just "there". A childlike faith of simply knowing Him grew into a time of deep theological study and debates and the splitting of hairs until thirty-some years later I find myself right back where I began: just knowing that God is "there".

The more I think that I know about God, the more I realize that I really don't know that much about Him. The paths that He has lead me on to release my grip on this world are not ones I would have taken if left to myself to decide. But those very paths have led me closer to Him.

On February 18, 2011, I experienced every mother's worst nightmare when God chose to take our 12-year-old son, Trent, home to heaven in a skiing accident. What I have discovered is that this same God has also been true to the promises that He declared in Scripture and has even allowed me to rejoice in His good works with Him. It still hurts and there are still tears, but I know that my Savior leads me and it is all for His glory, which ultimately brings me great joy.

To really do justice to tell this story, though, I must go back about twenty years. Back to the last month's of my father's life when God really started to get a serious hold of me and, unbeknownst to me, was already preparing me for this time in my life.

All those years ago, I was not saved. I had grown up going to church, vacation Bible school, and Bible camps. I knew plenty about the scripture, and would even pray on occasion when I needed something, but I did not have an intimate relationship with the God of the universe. It wasn't until just after I finished high school, when my Dad was diagnosed with lung cancer, that I really started to wonder about God. On that deathbed I literally watched God work right in front of my eyes. The memory still holds me captive as I try to understand the significance of those days.

My Dad wasn't the nicest of men. He left many in his past with more than hard feelings and bitterness. The beautiful part of this story, though, is that when God did save him in the last few weeks of his life the evidence was all the more real. I remember Dad's remorse over the people that he'd hurt along the way and how he invited them individually to come to his bedside. To the best of his ability, he expressed his sorrow over the pain that he had caused them. Most importantly, he shared with them about the saving grace of Jesus Christ. These words still ring in my ears as if they were spoken yesterday: "Terri, there is nothing more important than God."

In the midst of God taking my father from me those words didn't make much sense, but all these years later I find myself repeating them over and over again. God took Dad home to heaven only a few short months after the diagnosis. I remember the early morning that the family was called because it was thought to be Dad's last day. The feeling of peace and being "surrounded" was immense as he was about to be ushered into heaven. Dad was ready to meet his God, and happily passed away a short time later.

In those last few weeks, my Dad had also shared with me how grateful he was that God had let all of his fifteen children outlive him and that he never had to suffer the pain of a child dying. Watching my father die was hard enough; I couldn't begin to comprehend the death of a precious child. I held on to my fathers statement and adopted it as a personal fear, not realizing that it would be the one thing that I would refuse to give to God for the next twenty years.

My life, of course, went on. I half-halfheartedly sought this God of my father's. I prayed at meals like I had promised him I would do, and figured that was good enough. I tried reading the Bible, but the words didn't make any sense to me. I was a young woman in love, busily preparing for a wedding to Rob, my high school sweetheart. There wasn't much time or apparent need for thinking about such deep things.

Five years later, after our first daughter was born, I felt God's calling in my life again in a different way. Looking at the beautiful little girl that we had just been granted made me feel the weight and responsibility of choosing how to raise her. Deep within me I knew that it had to include God. When Alexis was just one week old I talked my sister into going to church with me. Eventually, Rob started attending church as well.

As it turned out, God graciously granted salvation to both Rob and myself within a year and a half. He started to change us dramatically, and to draw us closer to Him, through Scripture. God began teaching us to trust Him and gave us a desire to learn more about Him.

We had our "perfect" plan of having two children: a boy and a girl, please, God. Trent was born just two years after

Alexis. We were happy that God had gone along with our little ideas. But then along came Cole as a surprise in another eighteen months. After Cole, God called us to a special needs international adoption from India, and we welcomed Grace into our family. Five years later, we welcomed Micah home from India through another adoption. Man plans and God laughs. Thankfully, God has let us laugh along with Him.

The Boy

Chapter 2

⟨❦⟩

Before I was born the Lord called me;
from my birth He has made mention of my name.

Isaiah 49:2b

Trent's whole pregnancy was tough on me on every level.

Back aches from the start to the point that I could hardly get out of bed once in it. Emotionally, I wasn't ready to have another baby yet, and I was still chasing a spoiled little girl who had become my all in all. As I would tell Trent at the hospital after the accident: he was a bugger to bring into this world and a bugger to let go.

His birth was very long and difficult and painful. On March 10, 1998, when our first little boy was finally born, we rejoiced over this new creation. We counted his toes, oohed and aahed over how beautiful he was, kissed him, and held him tight, never wanting to let him go. We dreamt about the joy he would bring us as we praised our Heavenly Father for him, all the while entrusting God with his life. Rob was so proud of his new little boy (big boy, he was the biggest of our babies at 8 pounds 3 ounces) and kept stealing him from the nurses.

From his first checkup at a week old, Trent had ear problems that would affect him for years to come. Continuous fluid in his ears and numerous ear infections brought us to the doctor's office and emergency room several times. Finally, when he was nearly 2 years old, we found a doctor who encouraged us to have tubes put in his ears, which cleared everything up. By this time, though, Trent's speech was very delayed and we spent the next five years or so struggling with teaching him how to speak clearly. He always had an accent of his very own.

At an early age Trent had a desire to pray. When he was little we used to call him "the prayer warrior" because he would pray about everything. Couldn't find something, let's pray. Needed help doing something, let's pray. I can envision him squatting down at the bottom of the stairwell with his little hands folded, eyes squeezed shut, praying over something of utmost importance to a three-year-old.

Another trait that I saw developing at this time was anger. Even at that little age, the evidence that sin still ruled him was obvious. Frustration about simple things, especially his speech, would boil over into fits of anger. It was a deep anger that I prayed about and tried hard to help him control and gain victory over for years.

Also around this time an intense spiritual battle began raging over Trent's little soul. At the time I could not explain it, and have tried over the years to pass it off as meaningless, but I can still clearly recall many consecutive nights standing in his bedroom doorway and literally feeling the spiritual fight going on over him. Of course, as his mother, I prayed and begged God again and again for his salvation. After a certain point, and multiple nights of battling, I had the peace that washed over me with all certainty that God had won; Trent was His. I rejoiced then, of course knowing nothing of why such a battle would be fought over such a little boy and what the implications would be only eight years later.

I have prayed nearly every night for our kids' salvation, but never have I felt the same intensity since those days of praying for Trent. I always struggled to love him the same as the other kids and always thought that I was loving him too much for some reason. Looking back now I can understand just a little bit that it was because all of my earthly, motherly loving had to be poured into him in only twelve short years, and God was actually allowing me to love him more intensely for it while he was here. And love him I did.

It was many years later before God would choose to reveal salvation to Trent. Rob and I continued to do our best to raise him up to know the Lord, to make him aware of his own sinfulness, to lay out the gospel, to warn him to guard his thoughts and actions, and to be aware of his weak points that would allow sin to enter. We taught him Scripture, brought him to church, AWANA, vacation Bible school, and Bible camps. But instead of seeing fruit, we saw a hardness in his heart toward God. He grew in head knowledge, but when it came to knowing God he continued to refuse Him.

Rob has shared with me about the nights that he would tuck Trent into bed, pray him his blessing, and talk to him about salvation. He would ask Trent, "Do you know that you are a sinner?"

"Yes."

"Do you know that you're not right with God?"

"Yes."

"Do you know what God requires to enter heaven (perfection, but we can never be perfect because of our sin, therefore Jesus Christ had to come as a perfect sacrifice in our place and only by believing in Him can we be saved. Repentance of our sins and belief in Jesus leads to salvation, which is a gift from God alone)?"

"Yes."

"Do you want to repent and be saved?"

His response, said with a stone hard face, continued to be the same, "No." Absolute refusal to have anything to do with God's grace, even from an 8-year-old.

Scripture teaches that we are dead in our sins (Ephesians 2:1). A dead man cannot grab the life preserver that is thrown to him from the boat, just as a person dead in their sins cannot choose to be saved. Scripture also says that it is God who chooses us and causes us to be holy and blameless in His sight through Jesus Christ (Ephesians 1:4-5). Oh, how we longed for that day in Trent's life.

The head knowledge continued, as well as the sins that Trent could not control. He would struggle intensely with them and knew that they mastered him, but still he would not repent and accept God's grace. Until one evening in May 2010.

Everybody else had already gone to bed that night, except for Trent and I. We were sitting at the dining room table working on a sewing project. He loved to sit with me when I sewed. Early on, as a young boy, he had learned to cut the thread and piece together quilt squares as I chain stitched. I was intent on my sewing, and with the noise of the machine and the late hour, we were just happy being together without talking.

For some reason, I happened to look up and saw Trent's face in turmoil. He looked devastated over something.

I asked him, "Trent, what's wrong?"

Not a kid who would ever talk in the first place (believe me, I tried every tactic over the years and he was more stubborn than I am), it surprised me when he said, "Mom, I'm not right with God." I was speechless.

Rather than open my big mouth and lead him to a false conversion that was based on my words, I just took that 12-year-old boy into my lap and held him as he cried. I think I was probably crying a bit, too, marveling at what God was doing right before my eyes. Eventually I started reminding him of Scripture, reassuring him of what he already knew, of what God said about sin, repentance, and salvation. After quite some time we prayed together and he accepted Jesus Christ as his Savior. Oh glorious day!

Life went on as spring and summer became busy around our little farm. Trent was not perfect (just because a person receives salvation doesn't mean he stops struggling with sin), but fruit in his life was beginning to appear. He had the head knowledge, and God was transforming that into heart knowledge. He began to have little victories over sins he had struggled with, but still the anger reared it's ugly head on many an occasion. My own prayers went on for God's work as he fought the good fight (1 Timothy 6:12). Prayers for repentance of sins, relationships with his siblings, and that God would somehow use him in a mighty way for His glory.

Trent's own Bible reading time became more important to him, and, even though it was required to memorize Scripture for home school, he willingly chose to memorize additional verses as well. His questions at family devotions were full of insight, his knowledge of the Bible was ever deepening and curious, and his prayers were sweet words to my ears as I heard what God was doing in his young life. I can still see how his eyes lit up and twinkled as he talked about God and some new-found revelation in Scripture.

Alexis shared with us how Trent would come into the girl's room many nights after being tucked into his own bed. "First he would pick on Grace, then he would jump on my bed and tease me, but after he settled down our conversations always turned to talking about God." How I wish I could have recorded some of those conversations.

Later in the summer of 2010, Trent went with his youth group on a canoeing/camping trip for three days. I remember having a foreboding feeling about his going, contemplating, what if God takes him and he doesn't come home? Thus started the regular saying between the two of us:

"Trent, if God decides to take you first, do you know where you're going?"

"Yes, Mom. Love you," he'd say.

"Love you, too, Trent. See you when I get there, then."

The whole trip I constantly wondered where he was and what he was doing. Trent enjoyed spending time fishing on the river, so I comforted myself thinking about how much fun he was probably having. But that feeling of dread would not go away. I was so relieved to see him return home and just held him tight, feeling silly that I had worried over him so much. I have gotten much better at letting my kids "live" without being a hovering mother, but I am convinced looking back that God used that trip to prepare me for what was ahead: the day that Trent would leave with his youth group and never return home.

Summer turned into fall, and with it Trent heard about middle school football. Years ago we had participated in soccer with the boys, but after many practices of nobody being ready and not enjoying all the running, we gave up on organized sports. For some reason Trent was adamant about playing football and did a lot of sweet talking and buttering up in a way that only he could do to soften my heart. I finally gave in after seeing his determination. Looking back on it, I am so glad I did because it gave the family a reason to rally around him one last time for several weeks in a row.

To bless us for allowing him the privilege of playing football, he worked extra hard on his chores and home school, as well as encouraging the other kids to do the same, to make sure that everyone could get to practices on time. Trent enjoyed the sport and his coaches immensely, and he put everything he had into his practices and games. It was amazing to watch him grow in so many ways in those few weeks. My young boy was turning into a young man right before my eyes: physically, emotionally, and spiritually. It brought me great joy to watch how intensely he played the game and took the sport so seriously.

Trent's other love in life was hunting, with fishing coming in as a close second. Since he could first walk and talk all he wanted was to turn 12 years old so that he could carry his own gun. There wasn't much talk about him growing up other than the vague dreams of owning a huge deer ranch in Iowa where all the big bucks were shot on the hunting videos. And no way, no how, did any of his plans ever include a wife. We teased him that he would change his mind, especially if he found a woman that hunted and had her own gun and four-wheeler. He was confident, though, that he would never marry, just like he was confident that he would never have any use for learning how to play the piano. My own prayers for his spouse usually turned into prayers of contentment for Trent, rather than God preparing a young lady for him.

Trent lived life fully and enjoyed to the utmost the things that he loved. What he disliked (school, reading, writing, cleaning, or washing dishes) he put the least amount of effort into and was only excited to do them when there was gain for him, like earning time on the computer or getting outside to do something fun.

He loved to cook, though. He was always suggesting meal ideas like tacos, taco soup, sloppy joes, omelets, smoothies, oysters, shrimp, venison, any wild game he had shot, enchiladas and fruit. He loved to eat as much as he loved to cook; except for carrots and the beans in chili. His cooking was never bland, but always included extra spices to doctor it up and usually included fancy ways of serving or fancy china to serve it on. Breakfast in bed was another one of his "specialties" that we all enjoyed.

Maybe not by choice, but for the love of his mother, Trent was my barn helper. Although he wasn't always excited to help milk the goats, he was always excited to be at the barn when the kid's were born. During kidding season he would insist that I wake him up for middle of the night deliveries. He anticipated the new births as much as I did.

He was always right there helping out with all of the projects around the farm. Together we built the horse corral at the cabin sight, the arbors, the arena, the calf shed and the fences. I walk by and look at the chicken coop that the boys and I built and can envision him helping frame the wall, or climbing the rafters, or standing on the ladder to paint the high spots.

There are four walls of a log cabin standing in the horse pasture just waiting for a roof. Trent and Cole spent most of a summer chopping and hauling pine trees, building and stacking logs, and even installing a door and windows as the start of a boy's dream fort that Trent will never see completed.

I miss you, my son.

Fall turned into winter, and with extra bills due on the farm, Rob's hours being short at work, and several girls quitting or going on vacation, I found myself accepting work at the hospital nearly every weekend from November through February in my casual clerical position. I was on a four-day stretch of working from Tuesday through Friday the week of the accident. I was looking forward to having several weeks off in a row as the goats were due to deliver the following week. Rob and I had plans to work on finishing the barn remodeling project that weekend, and I could devote myself to being full-time wife, mother, teacher, and farmer for a while again.

The Friday before my work-week started, Trent and Cole were invited to spend the weekend at their best friends', Thomas and Samuel's, house for a Star Wars all weekend/all night movie fest. They came home very happy, and very tired. The kids heard at Sunday school that there was a youth group skiing trip coming up and were excited to go. After finding out that there were no girls going, Alexis decided not to go either. Rob called the youth pastor and got Trent signed up before filling out the paperwork so that everything was set for Friday morning.

The weather was beautiful that week. It warmed up to over 40 degrees, which is almost tropical for Wisconsin in February. On Monday, we were anxious to try tapping some maple trees to experiment with making our own maple syrup. Trent, always my willing helper, sidekick, and protector, came out with me and together we put some taps in the big maple tree in the middle of the pasture in the hopes that the sap might start to run early with the nice weather.

When I went to work on Tuesday, the kids stayed home with Alexis babysitting. Everybody had their list of responsibilities to take care of plus school to work on, which kept them happy and busy until I got home. Trent was the lunch man. I remember talking to him on the phone throughout the week as he reported the farm happenings and that there was no sap running yet.

On Wednesday, Rob was home with the kids. We all went to AWANA and SIGN at church that evening. Trent especially was having fun "protecting" Alexis from Julio and Jonah. They were all smiling and happy as they chased each other around the church: kids just being kids.

Thursday found me back at work again. The weather was still beautiful when I got home, so we all spent time down at the barn. I did some rearranging and simply enjoying of the goats; dreaming about the babies to come, the new calves, and all the spring farm plans. Just normal life with lots of my own dreams and expectations of the weeks ahead. The kids had fun playing up in the hay-mow and didn't even fight. There was such a joy and happiness in everybody that night.

I had washed clothes and set Trent's favorite new blue shirt in his cubby-hole so that it would be ready for him to wear the next morning for his skiing trip. After a pancake supper I headed up to bed early to read and rest in anticipation of one more long day at work.

The kids were, of course, not as tired as I was and were bouncing off the walls. Trent especially was very happy. I can still see his smile and his new short hair-do that Rob had just buzzed a couple of weeks earlier, and I can hear the excitement in his voice about the skiing trip in the morning. I see him opening my bedroom door to jump on my bed and say, "Goodnight Mom, love you," and checking on me to make sure that I wasn't hiding any cheese puffs, then giving me one last kiss. After Rob tucked him in bed and prayed him his blessing, I heard him sneak down the hall to go pick on the girls. I shut the light off and crawled under the covers, expecting every day of the rest of my life to have Trent to say goodnight to.

The Accident

Chapter 3

"For I know the plans I have for you,"
declares the LORD,
"plans to prosper you and not to harm you,
plans to give you hope and a future."

Jeremiah 29:11

I woke up early for work on Friday morning and got showered, dressed, and ready to go.

I was happy to be nearly done working at the hospital for the week so that I could get back to farm life. As I was about to head out the door, Rob was heading upstairs to wake Trent up for his skiing trip. The weather had turned cold, windy, and snowy, so I had half-hoped they would cancel the trip.

As I drove to work, my thoughts kept going back to a book that I had read several years ago written by a Christian woman whose son had been killed in a car accident on the way back from a youth group trip. I remember praying, "God, I don't want a story like that."

Work went fine. I chatted with the ladies in my little office about Trent going on a skiing trip on this cold, blustery day and wondered if he was staying warm. I thought about him often and prayed simple prayers for him. Rob had some errands to run with the other kids, otherwise they were just planning on enjoying our regular Friday pizza-and-movie night. Alexis headed over to babysit at a friend's house in the afternoon. Just another normal day.

I was in for a 13 1/2 hour work shift, which is not unusual in my position. After my day in scheduling, I headed back to the emergency room desk to sit with the new gal who was almost done with her training. There was a full moon that night, and those of you who work in healthcare know what a full moon means. It did not disappoint as our little ER had been busy all day and was chaos on every level at the time I got back there. There was a change of positions for the registrars and doctors, plus patients filling the rooms and checking in at the registration desk, and the phone ringing off the hook. The fact that I was the one who answered the phone a little before five o'clock to hear wailing on the other end was only from God.

I couldn't make out what the caller was saying at first. The sobbing person asked if this was Terri, and I said, "Yes. Who is this?"

The response was, "There was an accident."

"Who is this?" I asked.

More wailing, "It's your husband. It's Rob."

Still not able to make out the voice, and surrounded by confusion at the ER desk, my first thought was that it was a friend calling to say that Rob had been in an accident. Finally, I made the connection.

Scripture says that there is a peace that surpasses all understanding (Philippians 4:7). At that point I felt that peace flood over me. I knew. I asked him, "Is it Trent?"

He said, "Yes, there was an accident."

I said, "Do I need to come home?"

"Yes."

I hung up the phone, picked up my bag, and told my coworker that I had to go home. Somehow I remembered to clock out, then walked by the cafeteria where my Mom was working that evening and called her aside. I told her that I didn't know anything other than there had been an accident with Trent and I was going home.

As I drove home I prayed for Trent; for healing, for the doctors and nurses, and for those with him. But I knew that my prayers were in vain. I knew that there was no healing needed. God directed my prayers to be prayers for us, for strength, for peace. I can't say that I gave up praying for Trent's healing, or that I would give up praying until I heard that it was not needed, but on some level I knew what I would hear when I got home.

I walked in the door to wailing and simply asked Rob, "Is he alive?"

"No."

What happened next was only by God's strength, and is so much the way that He made me, because I didn't break down or wail with the rest of them. Rob, Cole, Grace, Micah, and I clung to each other, and in the midst of their crying I started singing, "What a Mighty God We Serve." I started praying out loud, asking God to help us, thanking Him for being God, and acknowledging that even this was His good and sovereign plan.

As I function best and clearest in chaos, my brain immediately went into check-list mode. The first thing we had to do was to have Christians surrounding and praying for us, then Alexis needed to get home and we needed to get to the hospital in Duluth, MN. We needed a bag packed, I had to call my Mom, and I had to call work, as I wouldn't be there on Sunday. And somehow I had to call my twin sister, Traci, and tell her so she wouldn't hear about it second-hand.

I picked up the phone and called our youth pastor, Jerry. He answered in his happy voice, asking how I was doing.

"Actually not so good, Jerry, we just found out that Trent died in a skiing accident. But listen to me, rejoice with me, we know that he is in heaven and we need to ask you to drive us up to Duluth."

After the initial shock, he said that he and his new wife, Ashlee, would be at our place as soon as they could.

God had all of this planned out perfectly as well, because it "just so happened" that a young couple from church was at their house for supper that night. By the time Jerry and Ashlee left their house, prayers were already being lifted up which would continue to carry us through the night and days to come. A prayer request was sent out on our AWANA church's email prayer chain simply asking for urgent prayers for our family. Our other church called their prayer chain with the news, and somehow a friend of Rob's sister heard about the accident while she was at a home school meeting. God ordained it that the whole group stopped the meeting and was in prayer for our family at the same time that we were arriving at the hospital.

The next call that had to be made was to get Alexis home from her babysitting job. Rob called Pastor Doug, as he already knew about the accident, and he quickly arranged to drop his wife off to babysit, picked up Alexis, and brought her home. We asked him to allow us to be the ones to share the news and comfort her. During the ride, Doug kept the conversation on suffering and God's purposes in them. As much as Alexis loves to talk about God and theology she was wondering why, in the first place, he wouldn't tell her why we needed her home, and why the conversation kept coming back to suffering.

As I was bustling around getting kids ready, packing a bag, and finishing details, Rob picked up Trent's Bible. The previous summer Alexis had bought some magnetic bookmarks with Scripture verses on them, and Trent had sweet-talked her into giving him one for his Bible. Rob looked to see where Trent had left off reading and found the bookmark in Isaiah 65. Verses 17-25 became the promises of God that would sustain us through the night, and many more days, months, and I am sure years to come, until God calls us home.

Isaiah 65:17-25 (NIV)

New Heavens and a New Earth

"See, I will create new heavens and a new earth. The former things will not be remembered, nor will they come to mind.

But be glad and rejoice forever in what I will create, for I will create Jerusalem to be a delight and its people a joy.

I will rejoice over Jerusalem and take delight in my people; the sound of weeping and of crying will be heard in it no more.

Never again will there be in it an infant who lives but a few days, or an old man who does not live out his years; the one who dies at a hundred will be thought a mere child; the one who fails to reach a hundred will be considered accursed.

They will build houses and dwell in them; they will plant vineyards and eat their fruit.

No longer will they build houses and others live in them, or plant and others eat. For as the days of a tree, so will be the days of my people; my chosen ones will long enjoy the work of their hands.

They will not labor in vain, nor will they bear children doomed to misfortune; for they will be a people blessed by the LORD, they and their descendants with them.

Before they call I will answer; while they are still speaking I will hear.

> The wolf and the lamb will feed together, and the
> lion will eat straw like the ox, and dust will be the
> serpent's food. They will neither harm nor destroy
> on all my holy mountain," says the LORD.

Shortly after reading the promises, Jerry and Ashlee pulled into our driveway. Thus began a relationship with two people who will be especially dear to me for the rest of my life. We had known Jerry for a couple of years as Alexis and Trent's new youth pastor at our AWANA church. He was a young man clearly gifted by God in teaching and preaching, as well as in striving to live every area of his life in obedience to God. We could see the depth in his understanding of the Bible, and appreciated his example and encouragement to the youth. On several occasions, we spent time in fellowship with him and were very excited when he met Ashlee and then soon after there was news of a wedding. She is such a sweet, God-honoring, young lady to accompany Jerry as he seeks after His Savior.

God put these two people in our lives for "such a time as this," to help set the foundation for how we would respond to what God was doing. He was so gracious to put this young couple in our lives that night to walk beside us and to hold up the Word of God to, and with, us. Jerry and Ashlee allowed us to be where God had us, which was trusting Him and rejoicing in His works. They encouraged us greatly. Of course, when they got to our home they joined us in our sorrow, giving hugs all around, and watching for ways to comfort.

When Alexis arrived, Rob broke the news to her. It took her a moment to register what he had said before the cry came. My first words were to share with her about witnessing Trent's salvation last spring. The expression on her face changed as she shared her own glimpses of watching God transform Trent's life and her own wondering if he had been saved then. As she realized that Trent was in heaven, her demeanor changed from crying to smiling. We read the Isaiah 65 passage again, finished our last minute preparations, then all stood together and prayed.

Pastor Doug chose to drive his car up to the Duluth hospital ahead of us. Jerry and Ashlee drove our van so that we could ride and process things, which was a blessing because I don't think at that point we would have been able to make it to the stop sign up the road.

Right away the conversation was about the accident, about God, and about Trent. Laughter was not very far behind the tears as we rejoiced that Trent was in heaven and we reminisced about his life. One of the first things I remember thinking in the van was how happy Trent would be that he didn't have to finish his dreaded school workbook. For years I had claimed as my home school mantra that the most important thing for our kids was that they were right with God. The rest of the curriculum paled in comparison, and as much as I had mouthed that saying, tonight it was so true. It didn't matter tonight if Trent knew his times table or if he could conjugate a verb. God had saved him and he was in heaven. That was all that mattered tonight.

Cole became solemn and realized that he was the big brother now. What a weight on his shoulders. Grace broke the mood by wondering, then, since Trent was in heaven and couldn't own his half of the Xbox anymore, did that mean she could have it? And who was going to wash the dishes and clean the kitchen on Monday's now? Oh Grace! My little realist! Our conversations soon turned again to Scripture verses about God's plans, God's sovereignty, and heaven.

About half way to Duluth Ashlee noticed that we were low on fuel, so Jerry pulled into a gas station to fill up. As we all headed into the store I looked at the four children in front of me. I had to mentally tell myself that this is how it would be from now on. No more counting five heads, no more looking for three boys and two girls, no more Ken-doll locks and a black and fluorescent snowmobile coat. Life would never be the same again.

Soon after returning to the van, I realized that we would have to walk into that hospital room and see Trent's body in just a matter of minutes. Working at an emergency room I knew a little bit about witnessing tragedy, about procedures and smells and curtains and doctors and tubes and weeping parents. The heavy dread of knowing why we were taking a trip to Duluth started to sink in. Talking about your son being in heaven is one thing, seeing the shell of his body is another. As we started seeing signs for Spirit Mountain the reality sunk in deeper.

But then came God.

Was this not the God who had given me peace to hear the news? Was this not the God who was already allowing us to trust Him for His plans? Was this not the God who had ordained all things for His glory? Was this not the God who was so gracious to have saved Trent?

Did I really believe all those verses about Him never leaving me or forsaking me? Did I really think that God would leave me when I got to that hospital room? Was I really thinking that I was doing any of this in my own strength? One step at a time.

We began to wonder about what Trent's body would look like. A skiing accident, a tree, a dead son. That was about all the story that we knew. Was he mangled? Was there head trauma that would prevent us from seeing him? Broken, twisted bones? Thoughts about what would have to happen in the next few days began to surface. How do you go about planning a funeral? Burial or cremation? How many days off can Rob get? What do you wear to your son's funeral? But ultimately, how are we going to walk into that room and see Trent's dead body?

The lights of Duluth loomed ahead. The hospital was closer. We followed Doug's car through stop-lights and exits and finally saw the hospital. The hospital where they tried so hard to overcome what God had planned for that day. The hospital where Trent's body lay in one of those rooms. The hospital where doctors and nurses and registrars had come to work for another day just planning to get through their eight or twelve hour shifts and then go back home to bed, not realizing what God had in store for them either.

My Son

Chapter 4

For I am the Lord your God
who takes hold of your right hand and says to you,
"Do not fear, I will help you."

Isaiah 41:13

I remember it was cold outside that night when we arrived at the hospital.

We found a patient parking spot in the outside ramp, headed for the elevators and pushed up, only to find out that we didn't need to go up, so we rode back down. Our little group walked down and around the steps and outside into the cold again to head across the street towards the emergency room doors. This was it, no turning back. It was still real.

There were several guards near the door and in the guard's booth. I wondered which one was waiting for us. The gentleman sitting inside to the left of the double glass doors greeted our group of five adults and four children. He introduced himself as the officer who had been at the scene since shortly after the accident. After leading us inside to a waiting area near a fish tank, he again verified that Rob and I were Trent's parents. He graciously continued to offer us his condolences and shared what he knew about the accident. Then he asked if we had any questions.

At this point I can only say that I felt a welling up of the Holy Spirit within me. This man in front of me had an eternal destination, just like Trent did. I knew that Trent was in heaven and nothing was going to bring him back. But this man . . . what if it had been him on that slope? Where would he be?

Rather than asking the typical questions or responding with an outburst of tears I simply looked him in the eyes and asked, "What if that had been you? Where would you be right now?"

His was the first of many puzzled faces that looked at me with confusion when I asked that question. "I'd be fine," he responded.

"But where would you be?" I asked.

He smiled the smile of one who holds a secret with somebody else and said, "Heaven."

"How do you know?" I insisted. What did I have to lose? That he might get mad at me, or on the other hand, he might get saved.

That smile again, and the simple words, "Because of Jesus."

The officer led us into a private family waiting room where we all took a seat on couches or chairs to wait for the doctor. A kind male nurse came in to offer his condolences for our loss. He shared what he knew and said the doctor would soon be in to talk to us. A quiet, young, Asian doctor walked through the door and sat down directly across from Rob and I. Knowing the trauma that is felt in losing a patient, especially a child, and imagining how hard it would be to face the family, I felt sorry for him to be put in this position tonight.

He shared from his medical point of view what had happened since the ambulance had come through the emergency room doors, and offered his apology for the loss of our son. Again, the Holy Spirit came welling up inside of me so that I could hardly stand to sit there without a smile on my face before I could ask him. Again, the absolute confirmation that Trent was in heaven according to God's promises in Scripture and knowing that nothing could bring him back. And again, the overwhelming thought that this man, too, had an eternal destination.

He finally asked us, "Do you have any questions?"

"What if that had been you tonight?" I asked. I will never forget his bewildered look.

"What?" he asked.

"What if that had been you who died tonight? Where would you be?" I asked again.

He hung his head and twiddled his fingers. I could sense the others in the room anticipating his response as much as mine.

"We all deal with these things differently," he finally said.

"Yes, we do, but where would you be? We know our son is in heaven because of what Jesus Christ did on that cross. Do you know where you would be?" I asked.

Again, he hung his head and looked down at his hands. "I will choose to keep that private," he responded.

I could respect that, but not without at least warning him. I told him that was fine, but that he would be in my prayers that he would know the saving grace of Jesus Christ. I also told him that it was not an accident that we had met tonight in this way, and that I hoped he would consider where he was with God. Relieved to be let off the hook, he said that he would go get the chaplain who would take us back to see Trent's body.

Now, those of you who know me personally know that I hold firmly to what Scripture teaches. How many times in the last several years have I gone on about women pastors and what I believe about the churches embracing of a practice and position that the Bible clearly lays out as a man's role? So, when in walks a female chaplain, I seriously thought about requesting somebody else, then realized that my sovereign God was in control of who walked in that door just as much as He was in control of Trent going down that hill.

We decided that Rob and I would go back first and see Trent's body and then the kids would be brought back. We took a right, a left, another left, and yet another left, before we came to the closed door with the rose card on it. Nobody met our eyes as we walked past. They knew who we were and why we were there. I have seen it from the other side of the desk before, and there isn't much you can say or do at that point. But what I hope those people saw that night was God shining through us as we walked the halls to enter that room, fully trusting God and His sovereign plan. The guard met us at the door and smiled. The chaplain opened the door and it was time to walk in.

The curtain was drawn and we knew that once we crossed into that hospital emergency room we would face our worst nightmare. Just inside the door Rob and I prayed together for the strength to go in. We acknowledged God's plan as being good and right because He had ordained it.

I walked in first and saw Trent's body lying there on the hospital bed. They had to leave a breathing tube in his mouth until the autopsy could be done. I remembered just a couple of weeks before when Trent and Cole had taken a tour of our emergency room with Paul, a registered nurse, and how he had shown them the variety of medical equipment and supplies. Amongst other things, he had talked to them about how to insert a breathing tube and why they would need to use one on a patient. What strange things go through your mind.

There was my son, but it was so clearly not Trent anymore. It was truly just a shell. A beautiful, young, 12-year-old shell of a body. I walked up to his left side and touched him.

"Where are you, Trent?" I asked.

It was so evident that there was no soul left. The body was beginning to turn cold and yellow already. There was no obvious evidence of trauma other than some scratches on his forehead, which weren't any bigger than he would have gotten playing out back with Cole or falling off his bike.

I hugged him and kissed him and stroked his hair. Like the night when he was born, I began to memorize every part of his body that I would soon never see again: his ears, the little mole between his eyebrows, his eyelashes, and his fingernails that he hated to cut. At the hospital this night, I marveled at him one more time. I uncovered his feet and kissed them, counting his toes. I took his hands out from under the sheet and held them. I caressed his beautiful face. I told him how much I loved him.

Not wanting to forget a single moment of this night, I intently looked at everything in the room. The sheet, the hospital gown, the cupboard doors, the sink in the corner, the chairs, the Kleenex box, the silent machines and monitors. This was a night that God had ordained and I did not want to miss a fragment of His detail.

I dug out the camera and asked Rob to take our final pictures together. I figured that if I never wanted to look at the pictures again I would never have to, but if I never took the pictures I would not have the choice.

Rob and I spent time alone with Trent. The whole twenty-three years that we have been together as a couple were wrapped up in this moment somehow. I would never have guessed that God would have this in store for two young teenagers in love all those years ago. This young boy, whose body was lying here, was a part of both of us. The person he was had been because of us. The pain that I felt, Rob felt; maybe even more so.

Soon the chaplain knocked and asked if we wanted the kids to come in. Alexis wept when she saw her brother's body. How my heart broke for her. Cole and Micah kept their distance. Grace soon chose to leave. We allowed them to be as much a part of everything as they wanted to be, explaining what would happen next and what we expected to help prepare them, but did not force them to stay longer or get any closer than they wanted to.

I had brought Trent's Bible along and read Isaiah 65:17-25 aloud again, rejoicing in the perfect work that God was doing right then in our midst in the emergency room; holding on tightly to the promises that He had given us.

More knocking, more interruptions, more questions. Did the kids want to go back? Did we need the chaplain? Could we answer a couple of questions? Did we need anything?

We could hear pages overhead on the intercom and machines beeping in the other emergency rooms. There were numerous patients living their own traumas on the other side of those walls. People were walking in the hallways; doctors and nurses and janitors just there another day to do their jobs as God was doing His.

At some point Rob and I were called away to the private waiting room again for a phone call about donating Trent's organs. We both immediately felt peace about offering whatever we could. To think of someone else's life becoming better because of our tragedy was an honor.

It was getting very late and everybody was tired by the time we got back to Trent's room. The ski resort had offered to rent us a hotel room if we wanted to spend the night in Duluth. We wouldn't be able to see Trent's body again once we left the hospital so we decided it was best to head home and wake up in our own beds.

The room cleared out so that our family could say our final goodbyes in private. The nurse brought scissors and an envelope so that I could cut some of Trent's spiked hair as a keepsake. I hugged my son's body one more time and kissed his beautiful face. Then I walked out the door and resolved not to look back, determining to trust God every step of the way for what He had planned, all the while longing to be in heaven myself.

The ride home was spent trying to absorb what God had just done, and what He was going to do. I really expected that if something like this ever happened in my life that it would be a surreal experience; like it really wasn't happening, like it was a dream. God allowed it all to be very real along with much clarity about everything that was happening while it was happening. Which, looking back, meant that I could accept it and live every moment of it without regrets. I was honestly rejoicing that Trent was in heaven and there was no pain of my loss yet.

Jerry said the words that I have held on to as I walk through this: "You will have to be careful to be honest with your thoughts and feelings." My family tends to be "stuffers" when it comes to feelings. I am a people-pleasing stuffer at my core. At that point, I was stuffing being happy that my son was in heaven because others might not understand it. Those words gave me freedom to be right where God had me right then, and for the months since, and probably for the rest of my life, wherever and however God has me. Freedom.

The rest of the ride home was spent talking about God and how good He is to us. Talking about Trent, talking about heaven, talking about the rapture, trying to sing "It Is Well With My Soul," by hymnist Horatio Spafford, with a mostly tone deaf family. I began to understand to a deeper level the first stanza:

> "When peace like a river, attendeth my way,
> When sorrows like sea billows roll;
> Whatever my lot, Thou hast taught me to say,
> It is well, it is well, with my soul."

Cole, Grace, and Micah fell asleep. At one point Jerry had to swerve to miss a raccoon. Oh, how we thought about Trent who would have been so excited to see it. And then, finally talking about the obvious, the van brakes had started to go out.

We arrived home around 2:30 in the morning, got our sleepy kids to bed, and crawled into bed ourselves, still praising our God and Savior for His sovereign plans in our lives.

The Celebration

Chapter 5

~❦~

Shout for joy, O heavens;
rejoice, O earth;
burst into song, O mountains!
For the Lord comforts His people
and will have compassion on
His afflicted ones.

Isaiah 49:13

Our society does not know what to do with death.
Even as Christians we do not always know what to do with death. The topic scares us. The shell of the dead body scares us. The afterlife scares us. It is much easier to avoid discussing the subject so that life can just go on like it always has. The death of an elderly person is acceptable enough, but the death of a 12-year-old boy is another matter.

In planning Trent's funeral God gave Rob and I the clarity to make tough decisions that we could have never dreamt of making. Trent died on a Friday afternoon. On Sunday afternoon we were sitting in the funeral directors office trying to answer questions about how many people we expected to attend (Umm . . . none, we weren't planning a funeral this week, thanks) and what picture we wanted to use for his memorial card. It was like preparing for a wedding in less than a week.

Which songs do you want that will honor your son's life and the God who ordained all this? What color of casket would you like? How many death certificates do you think you'll need and would you like to order "Thank You" cards? Yes, No, Maybe, I really don't know. Can we send you the check or do you need it before we can pick up our son's ashes? Somehow, in those two days (really 2 sleepless nights, one day full of company, half a day of church, and a quiet half hour to actually talk about it) God guided us through all of the decisions with clarity.

The only music that I really like is Johnny Cash or old hymns, and Johnny Cash isn't exactly funeral music. When Alexis suggested "Praise You in this Storm", by Casting Crowns, I had to look up the words on the Internet. When I read the chorus I knew we had to include the song in the celebration.

> "And I'll praise you in this storm
> and I will lift my hands
> for You are who You are
> no matter where I am . . ."

Perfect. So perfect.

Getting ready for church on Sunday, Alexis asked, "Mom, can I turn up the radio?" We have an ongoing battle over the radio volume in our house, but given the circumstances, I said "Sure." The song "Better is One Day in Your Courts", sung by Chris Tomlin, was blasting. Again, the words were perfect.

> "Better is one day in Your courts
> Better is one day in Your house
> Better is one day in Your courts
> than thousands elsewhere . . ."

Pretty much everything about the funeral was non-traditional. To start with, we chose to have no viewing the night before. I have been to too many viewings where people are crying and sad, and it is exhausting for the loved ones left behind. We chose to have a private viewing for our family first prior to the funeral, followed by a private viewing for the extended family, then open viewing and seating at 3:00 for the public. The celebration service was at 4:00, followed by supper and a final viewing.

It was our desire that the gospel be preached, and preached again, at Trent's funeral. We have two church families, so we asked both of our pastors to preach: Pastor Doug and our youth pastor, Jerry. In having the gospel preached first, those who were saved could rejoice with us that Trent was in heaven, and those who were not saved would be faced with the reality of death and eternity. We wanted to be able to minister to people on every level possible: hearing the word, singing and worshiping, reading Scripture and Trent's story (which went out in every bulletin) along with meeting their physical needs of being fed, hugged, and comforted.

There was a lot of smiling that day. Of course there were a lot of tears as well, but it was overall a day of rejoicing in God and His work. It was a celebration of God's salvation in Trent's life more than it was a funeral.

The odds of me being late to my own son's funeral are pretty good. Yes, you who know me personally are chuckling, so you can understand why we planned to be at the church a whole hour earlier than we were supposed to be. The girls wanted me to curl their hair, so after showers and putting on our new outfits, I curled and hair sprayed their hair. The boys, too, were in a hairspray-mode in honor of Trent's new spiky hair-do so they also got their hair all fancied up.

We drove to the church in the truck since the brakes had started to go out on the van on the way home from the hospital

Friday night. Ah, yes, this is a fallen world, which doesn't even stop to let you bury your son. I was doing all right until we pulled into the church parking lot and saw the hearse. I was actually glad to see the hearse parked because since it was parked it must have meant that they were all set up. In my mind I could handle them having everything set up, but I could not handle the unloading of the casket.

When we are weak, God is strong. He empowered us to walk through those church doors, and promised to be with us for it all. The anticipation for this celebration was so high in our family that day. We were so ready to publicly worship God for bringing Trent home to heaven and to share what He had been doing in our lives. Jerry and Ashlee greeted us with a hug, and then we chatted and finished a few last minute preparations. We talked with the funeral director and they let us know that they were ready for us to come into the sanctuary for our private viewing time.

Our family, and Jerry and Ashlee, all joined hands in a circle and spent time in prayer before we stepped foot into the sanctuary. Every one of us knew that it had only been the grace of God that had brought us this far, and considering what was to come (even just being able to walk into the sanctuary and seeing Trent's body again), we could only do the rest by His grace. We acknowledged God's goodness in His perfect plan yet again and asked Him for salvation for the lost who would hear the gospel that day. Knowing that God would lead us, we smiled and walked in to see Trent's body in the coffin for the first time.

It is strange how our bodies change after death. The boy who God had formed inside my own body, who I had so often carried and tenderly nurtured, hugged and kissed and snuggled and loved in his flesh was no longer in that flesh. The cold, hard body in that casket resembled my son, but the spirit who was Trent had been gone for nearly a week. The apostle Paul was right in calling these bodies mere tents. Scripture says that we are mortal creatures and that one day we will leave these bodies behind (2 Corinthians 5:1-10). When the Lord calls me home I will be more than ready to be rid of mine. After realizing how true God's Word was in this as well, we could rejoice once more that Trent was in heaven.

Jerry and Ashlee stayed close and honored our last private moments with Trent by being with us. Just as God sent Aaron and Hur to hold up Moses' arms so that the battle would be won, God sent people to hold up our arms during this battle. Jerry and Ashlee were two of the many that God sent.

Trent was never a formal dresser. He always looked so handsome in his maroon "church" shirt so we chose that along with a simple pair of khaki dress pants as his final outfit. To be true to who he was as a young boy, we also chose no socks and his high camouflage rubber boots, along with his favorite camouflage boxers; just the way we think he would have wanted to be dressed at his funeral.

At the meeting to discuss the funeral arrangements, the director had shown us pictures of fancy caskets with ruffles and silk and polished chrome to choose from. Rob and I just looked at each other across the table, and then Rob asked if they had a pine box. That must have been the point that the funeral director figured we had to be in shock (or else really cheap).

Rob continued to share with him that Trent would have built his own casket had he known that he was going to die this week and that neither one of us could picture him in something so floofy and frilly. Well, they figured they had something in the back room that would work. Hmm, what kind of casket would you pick for your funeral? Odd, odd things that we never thought we would have to decide for our son. We chose to drape the jean quilt he had made over the top of the coffin, along with a smiling picture that captured him so well, and his Bible open to the Isaiah 65:17-25 verses that God had given us the afternoon he died.

The next thing I did after seeing his body lying there in the coffin was to go get my hairspray bottle and fix his hair. Yes, he should have had a compassionate mother, but at this point we were so full of joy that he was in heaven and we were also elated at the opportunity to be able to tease him however we wanted to. What are families for if not to laugh at and with each other?

For years we had teased Trent about wearing his hair long in "Ken-doll locks". A couple of weeks before the accident he surprised us all and asked Rob to buzz him so that he could spike his hair. The transformation was amazing! He looked like a different kid. When he walked into weight lifting class for the last time, Coach Olson came up and introduced himself and wondered, "Who was this new boy?" And he wasn't kidding! I had teased Trent numerous times in those few days before the accident about using more hairspray than I did and that I was going to make him buy his own bottle the next week. So, smiling and laughing, I spiked up his hair and sprayed it with hairspray.

Another detail that I am so glad we thought of was to ask a friend to photograph the funeral for us. Because of Rhonda we have so many precious pictures to help us remember the day. Glimpses of the service that I would have never known about were captured through her lens; smiles and hugs, people we didn't get to see, and a row of young boys lined up in their football jerseys in honor of their friend were all memorialized in those photos.

As extended family started to arrive we greeted crying aunts and uncles, pancake eating cousins and giggling girl cousins, grandmother's and grandfather's, and our neighbor, Russell, who was like a grandpa to Trent. My soap opera family has 15 children, and soon several of them started coming in. Somehow, Rob ended up standing in as the door-man to give the family a bit of privacy as the public started arriving. Together we were able to greet people prior to the funeral and share our hope and joy with them.

The shocked, confused faces that saw us smiling were only more encouragement to share why we were so happy. As with the first people we saw after Trent died we asked, "Where would you be if you had died on Friday?" Not letting them go until they could answer one way or another. We encouraged the saved to rejoice with us because Trent was in heaven, and warned the unsaved that they may not have tomorrow to decide. Settle today what God is calling you to settle.

Fifteen minutes before the service started somebody came to get the family to meet in Jerry's office to pray. Pastor Doug was sitting in a chair with a downcast look. I took his face in my hands and said to him, "Rejoice with us! Trent is in heaven! What have you taught us for the past fifteen years? Then rejoice with us!"

Jen was also there as she was going to bless us with her beautiful voice by singing a solo. She was so nervous (I can understand why), so we encouraged her that if God was faithful with all the rest of the details that He would be faithful with her voice as well. We prayed for her to sing beautifully and clearly, and above all else we prayed for salvation for all who would hear the gospel message, some for the first time.

We walked out of Jerry's office and through the dining room full of sad people. The church entryway had been full when we tried to get through to Jerry's office, so I had just assumed that they were waiting to get into the sanctuary. Little did I know that the sanctuary seats were full, it was standing room only, and not just the dining room, but even the back room of the church was full. The outpouring of love from our little community was so overwhelming, and has been such a blessing to our family.

The service started with a welcome and prayer, followed by Jen singing the song "Untitled Hymn", by Chris Rice. It is a song that Alexis had sung at church before, and it is one of my favorites. The words were so perfect for this day and Jen's voice was flawless singing it. I could hardly look at her because it was so beautiful and fitting as I considered what God had just done in our lives. The final stanza made me praise God and His work and brought tears to my eyes:

> "And with your final heartbeat
> Kiss the world goodbye
> Then go in peace and laugh on Glory's side
> and fly to Jesus . . . fly to Jesus and live!"

After the solo, Pastor Doug preached the gospel message and read the Isaiah 65:17-25 passage aloud. Next we chose to have the whole congregation stand and join in singing worship songs. It was especially an honor that one of the young men who had been helping with Trent's youth group was there to play drums with the worship team. Trent had looked up to Seth and enjoyed learning about God with him. What a beautiful time of worship and praising God with hands lifted for His good works! The worship started with "Here I am to Worship", lyrics by Tim Hughes, followed by "Praise You in this Storm", and "Better is One Day in Your Courts".

> "So here I am to worship,
> So here I am to bow down,
> So here I am to say that You're my God . . ."

We truly were there to worship God for His salvation and His good works. My heart overflowed with praise to my Savior for bringing Trent to heaven, and the songs were only a tiny outpouring of that gratefulness.

Worship was followed by Jerry's sermon. It was the gospel message preached again, seasoned with love, grace, and much hope and rejoicing.

At the end of the sermon I was surprised to hear Jerry ask Rob to come up to say something. The night before the funeral Jerry had asked me how we wanted to end the service. My brain was on overload and I couldn't come up with any better suggestion than to say that we would have to leave that up to God, too, and that I would trust Jerry to decide what seemed best at the time. Just before the service Rob had talked to Jerry and told him that if he felt led to get up and talk that he would give Jerry a thumbs up or thumbs down to let him know.

Rob is not a public speaker, but the gospel message that God proclaimed through him was crystal clear and so beautiful and honoring to what God was doing. If there had been a single dry eye in that church building they would have been crying at this point to see Trent's father up there praising his God for taking his son to heaven.

To end the service we chose to have the congregation join in singing "It Is Well With My Soul" as the final hymn.

Again (thumbs up), Jerry called Rob up to close the service. Rob led us in prayer then offered up a blessing for the congregation. It is a blessing from Numbers 6 that he has prayed at bedtime for the kids for several years, and one that Trent requested every night without fail.

"May the Lord bless you and keep you.
May the Lord make His face shine upon you,
and be gracious to you.
May the Lord lift up His countenance upon you,
and give you peace.
In Jesus name, Amen."

Our family had been sitting at the head of the open casket. At the end of the beautiful service we stayed right where we were, and Rob and I spent the next three and a half hours ministering individually to every person who came through the receiving line to see Trent's body one last time. Afterward, Rob and I shared with eachother that we both felt led to only focus on the person directly in front of us, not to worry about rushing the line through or who was next, but to take the time and meet the needs of the individual who was in our presence.

Whether it was asking where would they be, challenging them, encouraging them with Scripture, rejoicing with them, dancing with them, (one of my favorites) tagging Trent so that he would be "It" forever, crying with them or just hugging them. God poured Himself out through us as we celebrated what He had done and what He promised to continue to do. There were many tears, and much repentance. We prayed that there was also salvation taking place.

Others told us of the people waiting in the line, encouraging and ministering to each other asking, "What if it had been you?" We had no idea of the still overflowing dining room or that there were so many people that they ran out of food. We were so honored to be used to share God's Word with so many that night.

When the crowd thinned (and we could have happily stood there all night ministering by God's strength) we found ourselves surrounding the coffin and laughing. Rob's sister's family and some of the younger girl cousins and friends had gathered around and we all got to talking about the rubber boots that Trent was wearing. The girls thought we were kidding, so we lifted up the sheet and bent over to look under the casket lid and everybody had to come and see. It turned into more laughter when we shared that the whole family was wearing color-coded camouflage underwear (or as close to it as Walmart sells this time of year) as one last, final connection as a family. Telling "Trent stories" brought yet more laughter, and we all pretty much agreed that he was the lucky one and that we would miss him like crazy.

As the sanctuary was finally quieting down, I took my last private moments with Trent as his Mother. I looked at that handsome face one more time, kissed him on the little mole between his eyebrows, and told him that the next time I would kiss him would be in Glory. In faith, I turned and walked away, knowing that my Savior would lead me. What a mighty God we serve.

The Releasing

Chapter 6

The Lord is close to the brokenhearted
and saves those who are crushed in spirit.

Psalm 34:18

I'd never really had to decide what my thoughts were on cremation before.

I guess I never really cared for the idea, but then again, I never had to make the decision before whether I wanted to have a loved one cremated or buried. To think back over the past events in our lives, and to ponder the decisions that we have had to make, I can only credit God with the clear understanding of how we were able to make any of them.

On the way up to the hospital the night of the accident, Rob and I had pretty much already decided that rather than a burial we wanted to have Trent's body cremated. Seeing his shell at the hospital and knowing that there was no soul left made the decision seem easier yet. With time to discuss it over the next couple of days before we had to meet with the funeral director, we both agreed that we did not want his body to be left in a grave, at some place that he never was, and take on the feeling of obligation to kneel down before it. It was a very freeing thought to not have his body tied here to this earth where we would be so tempted to leave it attached to this world rather than releasing every part of him to be in heaven where his soul was.

Part of the cremation process is deciding what to do with your loved one's ashes. Trent's birthday was on March 10, just three weeks after the accident. Three years ago we took a trip to Bass Pro Shops for his golden birthday and we had always told him that we would take a trip back down there someday. As a family we decided to make the trip with Trent's remains to Springfield, Missouri, and release his ashes along the way in places that would honor who he was and what he loved during his short time on this earth.

The first place on the list was our favorite Bible camp, which has been a central part of our family for years. As a child I attended the youth camps, and together as a family we have enjoyed camping there for several years. Our home-school schedule was based around going to family camp: we planned to be finished before Memorial Day weekend, summer ended and school started again after Labor Day family camp. We also saved money throughout the year that was earned from answers tallied by Dad during our family devotions, which we then used to splurge at garage sales on the drive up to camp. They are much anticipated, long weekends of total indulgence in spending time together while being surrounded by other Christians and eating lots of good food.

When Trent was only four years old he was fearless and climbed the thirty-foot rock tower and jumped down the zip line for the first time on their high ropes course. Many years followed that he continued to enjoy the high ropes courses along with paintball, swimming, boating, bocce ball, carpet ball, night-time black-light dodge ball, being first in the food line, friends, speakers, and campfires.

Since so many of our cherished family times have been spent at camp, we contacted the director and asked if we could spend some time with the staff who are like family as well as release some of Trent's ashes from the top of the zip line tower. I guess there has never before been a request made like that at camp, but Brian was happy to entertain us and welcomed us up for the afternoon. It's hard to know if you should be happy to take a trip to camp to release your son's ashes, or be sad, or somewhere in the middle. God chose to give us great joy and excitement as we headed out that sunny Tuesday morning.

It was wonderful to pull up at camp and to see all the familiar faces of the staff that we love so much. I wasn't sure, again, if I could get through this one-more-thing without losing it emotionally, but then Kristen walked out of the lodge and gave me a great big hug. She told me that she had gone up to the tower that morning and had prayed over the place, asking God to move in a mighty way that day. Again, I was reminded that God's plans are perfect, even in this. His strength is sufficient, especially when mine is weak (2 Corinthians 12:9).

Time was spent sharing with the staff about how good God had been to us, and then we all headed up through the snowy woods to the ropes course. After the staff got our family harnessed up, we took the winding, inside stairs up to the top of the climbing tower. Brian and our family stood on the platform overlooking the trees and the camp and we spent time in prayer, praising God and acknowledging Him for His good works. Again, we proclaimed our trust in His plans for His children.

To see my son's ashes in a bag inside that black box that Rob had picked up from the funeral home the day before was difficult. To think about putting my hand into that plastic bag and holding those ashes was more difficult yet. But, like everything else, I determined to go straight through it (versus going around, stuffing, side-stepping, coming back and grieving over it in twenty years) with God's strength. With a smile on my face I reached inside that bag, filled up my hand with gray ashes, flung them over the edge of that tall tower, and released Trent's remains. Then more and more and more.

Go in peace, Trent. We will not hold you here.

I could just imagine Trent standing up there with us getting ready to jump off fearlessly in a swan dive down the 200-plus-foot zip line. If I could have, I would have jumped fearlessly down the zip line that day, too, just so I could feel God catch me in that harness. It would have only been more proof to myself that He will catch us wherever He leads us.

Slowly, we made the descent back down the narrow stairs and were embraced by our camp staff friends again. There was a bit of time left to share and encourage each other before we had to head out for the next part of our trip. A big snowstorm had been predicted and we hoped to make it to Iowa before it hit.

Trent loved hunting! There were few things in his life that he enjoyed as much. In the last few months of his life he talked often about how he wanted to go deer hunting in Iowa. He had proclaimed that if he ever moved it would be to a big plot of land in Iowa because the hunting was supposed to be so good.

Iowa?? I always envision Iowa as corn fields, family reunions, and childhood memories of vacations to Uncle Evert and Aunt Eva's house on the lake. But to honor Trent's love for Iowa we determined to find a place to spread his ashes in that beautiful state.

On the drive down to Missouri for Trent's golden birthday trip we had seen the signs for the covered bridges in Madison County and had talked about going back to visit them one day. Wednesday afternoon, as we drove through Madison County again, I brought up the idea that we could release some of his ashes from one of the bridges.

Now, just for the record, lest you think that we are one big happy family all the time, I have to make a note here that this thought did not receive unanimous cheers. There were those in the van who were concerned about time and miles and distance, and those who just wanted to get to the pool. And then there were those who wanted Trent's ashes released somewhere that would have deer and turkey because, after all, Trent wanted to move to Iowa for the hunting, not the bridges. After a bit of debate, the decision was made to see just how far away the bridges were. If they were close enough, we would stop on the way down rather than on the way home.

After finding a map, and looking at our different options, we decided to try to find the Roseman Bridge. We drove along over several picturesque, snow covered back roads before we came to the quiet little bridge. It turned out to be just the kind of place that Trent would have loved. There was a river with beautiful woods surrounding it and even turkey and deer in the fields along the way. We all spent some quiet time sparingly releasing his ashes where we individually chose and then enjoyed the historic sight together.

The next stop on the trip was Springfield, Missouri. It was pretty late in the evening by the time we got into Springfield and we were all fairly tired from the long drive. Turning onto Sunshine Street again hit both Rob and I pretty hard as we remembered the excitement from our previous trip when Trent was with us. We easily found the hotel, and after spending some time crying in the bathroom, I finally put my swimsuit on and we all headed down to the pool. Alexis did a belly flop into the water, came up, and said "Trent, that was for you!"

On Thursday, the day of Trent's birthday, we headed over to Bass Pro Shop and relived the excitement of seeing the magnificent store once again with all of its hunting and wildlife exhibits. When we walked into the front entrance three years ago, the seven of us just stood there in awe, jaws dropped, looking at all of the amazing displays. On this day the six of us did the same thing. But this time I had my hand in my vest pocket holding onto my little bag of ashes, loving God for how He had planned everything out, and being honored to have a son in heaven.

The week after our trip, I took a quiet walk around our little farm and spread some remaining ashes. I visited the places that held so many precious memories with Trent: the maple tree, the cabin sight, the boys' fort, the pond. The tears flowed and the praises continued in my private goodbye to this boy with whom I was granted only twelve short years as his mother.

Farewell my son. Love you. Just like I told you all those times when you were still here on this earth, "If you go first, I'll see you when I get there."

Part 2

Grief and God

His Ways Are Not Our Ways

Chapter 7

*"I am the Lord; that is my name!
I will not give my glory to another
or my praise to idols."*

Isaiah 42:8

Sovereignty. God's sovereignty.

It's pretty hard to deny it if you spend much time at all in Scripture. This Word, this God, whom our human minds cannot fully comprehend, says in His Bible that everything in heaven and on earth is under His control and is also determined by His plan. *Easton's Bible Dictionary* states that the sovereignty of God is "His absolute right to do all things according to His own good pleasure."

Scripture clearly lays out that God is sovereign over His creation, over kings and kingdoms, over salvation, and even over the day of our birth and the day of our death. Daniel 4:17 proclaims God's sovereignty by saying:

> The decision is announced by messengers, the holy
> ones declare the verdict, so that the living may know
> that the Most High is sovereign over all kingdoms
> on earth and gives them to anyone He wishes and
> sets over them the lowliest of people.

First Chronicles 29:12 echoes Daniel in proclaiming God's sovereignty: "Wealth and honor come from You; You are the ruler of all things. In Your hands are strength and power to exalt and give strength to all." Job 14:5 pinpoints God's sovereignty over our very days: "A person's days are determined; You have decreed the number of his months and have set limits he cannot exceed." And Psalm 62:7 reveals God's sovereignty over salvation: "My salvation and my honor depend on God; He is my mighty rock, my refuge." Isaiah 45:7 says: "I form the light and create darkness, I bring prosperity and create disaster; I, the LORD, do all these things."

God's sovereignty is revealed first-hand as we look at the life of Joseph (Genesis chapters 37-50) and follow along from birth to death of a man who God chose to use to save the nation of Israel from a great famine. The path that Joseph was taken on to get to that position was full of pain, betrayal, temptation, and even prison. God's ways are usually not easy, but they do fulfill His plans for His glory.

What Joseph came to understand was that it was God who had ordained every step of the way. It would be my guess that at first it was difficult to see God's plan while he was in the pit where his brothers had thrown him, as well as in Potiphar's house, and then in the cold cell of the prison. There must have been many moments of struggling, but by the end of his life, Joseph gave all the credit and glory to God. He came to know that even though his brothers had intended to harm him, God had intended the path of his life for good. Joseph would have said along with Paul, "All things work for the good of those who love God" (Romans 8:28).

If God is sovereign over a man named Joseph, whose life is recorded in the Bible, isn't God also sovereign over our lives? If God ordained the beginning, the middle, and every detail until the end of Joseph's life, then isn't it easy to conclude that He has ordained every detail in our lives as well?

The life of Jesus is another example of God's sovereignty. There are claimed to be over 450 fulfilled, Biblical prophecies that point to Jesus being the promised Savior. The prophecies speak of who He is and what He would accomplish, both in His first coming and in His second. So many details of the life that God ordained for Him to live on this earth, and proof that He was the Messiah for whom His children were waiting.

Little details like where and how He would be born (Micah 5:2; Matthew 2:1-6), who would precede Him in His ministry (Isaiah 40:3-5; Matthew 3:1-3), how He would be betrayed (Zechariah 11:12-13; Matthew 26:14-16) and crucified (Isaiah 53:5; Luke 23:33) only to rise again (Psalm 16:10, 49:15; Mark 16:6-7), right down to the kind of drink that He would be offered (Psalm 69:21; Matthew 27:34) before He spoke His last words (Psalm 31:5; Luke 23:46). Little details that could never have been guessed hundreds of years before His existence and written down, but could only be more proof that points to a sovereign God who has all things planned out.

This evidence of God's sovereignty, then, begs the question: Why has God ordained all things? Scripture says that it is for His glory (Ephesians 1:11-12; Isaiah 43:7) God's glory is His beauty, His splendor, His very Self that is portrayed through His works. Great honor and praise is due to God simply because of who He is.

And why is God worthy of glory? Because He alone is eternal and the true God, He alone is the source of all life, He has unlimited power and wisdom which makes Him worthy of worship.

God is the Creator of the universe. The central purpose of everything that was created is to display the glory of God and all of His attributes: His splendor, His beauty, His love, His justice, His mercy, His kindness, His truth, His patience, His creativity, His salvation . . . The list could continue on and on. God alone is worthy because of who He is. God alone has absolute authority and possesses all power.

Scripture says that there is none like Him (Revelation 4:11; Psalm 113:5), none who is worthy of the praise, glory, and honor due Him simply because of who He is. He is the Creator, we are the created. He is the Potter, we are the clay (Isaiah 64:8).

Many, then, would ask: "How does the death of a 12-year-old boy bring glory to God?"

We have had people shake their fist, ultimately at God, as they heard us give Him the glory for taking Trent to heaven at such a young age. "What kind of a god would let a 12-year-old boy die?" they wondered. I would wonder, too, at the kind of god who would watch a 12-year-old boy die in a skiing accident and could not do anything to prevent it.

Connecting the dots of Scripture, though, clearly lays out a sovereign God with all power and authority to do what pleases Him for His purposes (Isaiah 46:10b). Purposes that we cannot always see or understand. Purposes that may have to wait until eternity to be answered. Purposes to advance His kingdom, to grow His children and draw them nearer, to answer prayers, and to grant salvation. Even purposes for a 12-year-old boy to die in a skiing accident.

What if His purposes included making the riches of His glory known to His children (Romans 9:23)? What if suffering is the very thing that God uses so that we will not continue to look for our comfort in this world that is temporary? What if God uses those very things to open our eyes to see beyond this fallen world so that we would consider our own eternity? What if struggles are the only thing that would create in us a longing for God Himself and our heavenly home?

What if every trial here would somehow reveal God's glory all the more throughout eternity? What if God has a master plan that we cannot understand and He only asks us to trust Him in it? Are you willing to trust Him even when you cannot see Him?

God does not want His children to be comfortable here in this world of the enemy. If that can only be accomplished through painful trials then we, as God's children, can find it easier to praise Him for them.

Paul says in Philippians 1:29, "It has been granted to you on behalf of Christ not only to believe on Him, but also to suffer for Him." Granted means gifted. Suffering, then, is a gift from our Heavenly Father. What an odd concept in our culture of ease and the pursuit of happiness. Why would God choose such a peculiar gift for His children? Why would He want His beloved to experience pain?

Because it is the only way to know Him deeply.

Psalm 119 clearly reveals God's sovereign hand in suffering. King David acknowledges God's hand in his own afflictions, and even praises Him for them.

> Before I was afflicted I went astray, but now I obey your word . . . It was good for me to be afflicted so that I might learn your decrees . . . I know, O Lord, that your laws are righteous, and in faithfulness you have afflicted me . . . If your law had not been my delight, I would have perished in my affliction (Psalm 119:67, 71, 75, 92).

First Peter 1:2 says that the elect "have been chosen according to the foreknowledge of God the Father, through the sanctifying work of the Spirit, for obedience to Jesus Christ." True salvation includes sanctification, and sanctification is hard work—hard work with unimaginable eternal rewards. It involves suffering and the continual dying to self; it grows our character and makes us persevere, as well as increasing our hope and our longing for God and heaven.

Sanctification is an action word. It is the setting apart of something, or someone, that is intended to be used for sacred purposes; to make holy; to purify. A true Christian is in a continuous state of being sanctified. Hebrews 12:7-11 tells us:

> Endure hardship as discipline; God is treating you as His children. For what children are not disciplined by their father? If you are not disciplined—and everyone undergoes discipline—then you are not legitimate, not true sons and daughters at all. Moreover, we have all had human fathers who disciplined us and we respected them for it. How much more should we submit to the Father of spirits and live! They disciplined us for a little while as they thought best; but God disciplines us for our good, in order that we may share in His holiness. No discipline seems pleasant at the time, but painful. Later on, however, it produces a harvest of righteousness and peace for those who have been trained by it.

God loves His children, but He will not leave them where they are spiritually. He will continue to grow them in righteousness. He has always set His chosen ones apart and called them to live a life different from the ways of the world. We are not to be of this world, but rather are to be transformed by the renewing of our minds through Scripture (Romans 12:1-2). Christians do not belong to this world, but to a heavenly kingdom that the world does not understand. God grows us closer to Himself, and reveals His glory, as we trust and live in His ways even— and especially—through trials.

In Isaiah 48:10-11 God says:

> See, I have refined you, though not as silver; I have
> tested you in the furnace of affliction. For My own
> sake, for My own sake, I do this. How can I let
> Myself be defamed? I will not yield My glory to
> another.

The purpose of refining is to remove all impurities, with the end result being a polished and perfect product. Refining is precise work. It only comes about with pressure, heat, and stress applied by the hands of a master silversmith. Rather than the end result being a shining metal object, God chooses to refine His children for His own glory, and He accomplishes that through suffering.

Through suffering our faith is proved genuine and results in praise and honor when Jesus Christ is revealed (1 Peter 1:3-9). God has chosen His elect to be tested and purified for the very purpose of revealing Himself in them. As we go through the fire of trials, God causes us to depend on Him alone. He draws us near, and reveals Himself through the refining process.

In Zechariah 13:9 God says:

> This third I will put into the fire;
> I will refine them like silver
> and test them like gold.
>
> They will call on my name
> and I will answer them.
>
> I will say, "They are my people,"
> and they will say, "The Lord is our God."

God has also ordained that the gospel will have the most effect when it is presented alongside suffering. Suffering reveals the fallen world that we live in. It shows us again and again that all is not right here, and it makes us long for God to make it right. In suffering the loss of a loved one, the thought of eternity is presented to many. Especially in the loss of a child, the cruelty of this world is seen clearly; the expected can no longer be expected. Our ideals of living long lives and then committing ourselves to Christ once we are done having fun are suddenly dashed. People are woken up to the fact that young age does not protect them from death.

Salvation itself included suffering. Jesus Christ was not spared suffering to bring salvation, so why, as His followers, do we think that we will avoid suffering? God determined that suffering would be a part of His plan for salvation and for sanctification. Hebrews 2:10-11 says:

> In bringing many sons and daughters to glory, it was fitting that God, for whom and through whom everything exists, should make the pioneer of their salvation perfect through what He suffered. Both the one who makes people holy and those who are made holy are of the same family. So Jesus is not ashamed to call them brothers and sisters.

Peter goes even further and tells us to rejoice when we suffer: "But rejoice inasmuch as you participate in the sufferings of Christ, so that you may be overjoyed when His glory is revealed" (1 Peter 4:13). We are called to join in on this suffering. Paul says, "Join with me in suffering, like a good soldier of Christ Jesus" (2 Timothy 2:3), and "So do not be ashamed of the testimony about our Lord or of me His prisoner. Rather, join with me in suffering for the gospel, by the power of God" (2 Timothy 1:8). Philippians 4:4 says, "Rejoice in the Lord always. I will say it again: Rejoice!"

How could Paul, who for the sake of the gospel message he preached had a history of being beaten, jailed, and even stoned nearly to death, so easily encourage believers to rejoice? Could it be because his joy was found in the Lord Jesus alone? Could it be because he found something that the world could not offer? Or, rather, God gave him something that the world could not offer? Could it be because he knew that nothing mattered more than Jesus and he understood that somehow, someway, someday God would make it all worth it (1 Corinthians 15:58)?

There is a certain peace and joy experienced by God's children who have suffered great things. It is the peace and joy of God Himself. In the midst of our pain and suffering it is something that I would not trade to go back to "normal". The hope of God is only stronger and greater in me because of the death of my son. This world no longer holds anything that satisfies, and only God brings joy. That alone is worth enduring all things, and yes, even worth rejoicing in.

Scripture says that the world we live in right now is the fallen world (Genesis 3). This world is the sinful world. In God's sovereign plan, man had to fall so that the glory of God could be revealed to it's fullest. Sin lead to pain, and ultimately to death. The whole world was thrown into the chaos caused by sin so that not only man, but the very earth itself, groans in longing and anticipation for the Savior to make all things right again (Romans 8:18-23).

Jesus promised that all would be made right, but He did not say that it would be made right in this world. Hebrews 11 is full of people who longed for God to make things right in their day, but who were also willing to wait for His timing. By faith, these people embraced God's word, trusted His testing, His leading, and His ways, even though none of them received what had been promised to them on this side of heaven. They had confidence in what they hoped for, and great assurance in what they could not see. For these things, they were commended. Our God is a just God and will make all things right in His time.

Scripture makes it clear that all of those things done for the glory of God in this world will result in God's richest rewards in heaven (Matthew 16:24-27). Somehow, unclear to us now, the gift of faith that is only from God will have eternal rewards beyond measure or earthly comprehension. As if dwelling in heaven with Jesus wasn't enough, God will reward His children for an eternity simply for believing what He said and living in that belief.

The Bible is very clear that there will be a judgment day. As believers, our salvation is secure in Jesus Christ's work on the cross. The refining fire of judgment will reveal the believer's work. First Corinthians 3:12-15 says:

> If anyone builds on this foundation using gold, silver, costly stones, wood, hay or straw, their work will be shown for what it is, because the Day will bring it to light. It will be revealed with fire, and the fire will test the quality of each person's work. If what has been built survives, the builder will receive a reward. If it is burned up, the builder will suffer loss but yet will be saved—even though only as one escaping through the flames.

Take a serious look at your own life. Are you building with gold, silver, and the costly stones of Scripture, belief, trust, and obedience? Or are you chasing the world fully and Jesus halfheartedly, thus building with wood, hay, and straw? Will your life withstand the fire of God's judgment? Are you ready for that day? If only what is done for Christ will last, then let us live our lives with no regrets for when we get to heaven. Let us strive all the more to advance His kingdom and work to build eternally rather than worldly, bringing as many lost souls with us as we can.

Do you believe what Scripture says, Christian brother and sister? Can you simply trust that the God who ordained the words will be true to them? Will you be patient and trust Him to fulfill them in His time? If so, then let His children walk in His ways, not in the ways of the world.

Isaiah 6:3
"Holy, Holy, Holy is the Lord Almighty; the whole earth is full of His glory."

Romans 8:28-30
"And we know that in all things God works for the good of those who love Him, who have been called according to His purpose. For those God foreknew He also predestined to be conformed to the likeness of His Son, that He might be the firstborn among many brothers. And those He predestined, He also called; those He called, He also justified; those He justified, He also glorified."

Ephesians 1:11-14
"In Him we were also chosen, having been predestined according to the plan of Him who works out everything in conformity with the purpose of His will, in order that we, who were the first to put our hope in Christ, might be for the praise of His glory. And you also were included in Christ when you heard the message of truth, the gospel of your salvation. When you believed, you were marked in Him with a seal, the promised Holy Spirit, who is a deposit guaranteeing our inheritance until the redemption of those who are God's possession—to the praise of His glory."

Hebrews 10:35-39
"So do not throw away your confidence; it will be richly rewarded. You need to persevere so that when you have done the will of God, you will receive what He has promised. For in just a very little while, 'He who is coming will come and will not

delay. But my righteous one will live by faith. And if he shrinks back, I will not be pleased with him.' But we are not of those who shrink back and are destroyed, but of those who believe and are saved."

Philippians 1:12-14
"Now I want you to know, brothers and sisters, that what has happened to me has actually served to advance the gospel. As a result, it has become clear throughout the whole palace guard and to everyone else that I am in chains for Christ. And because of my chains, most of the brothers and sisters have become confident in the Lord and dare all the more to proclaim the gospel without fear."

Isaiah 65:17
"Behold, I will create new heavens and a new earth. The former things will not be remembered, nor will they come to mind."

Revelation 21: 1-7
"Then I saw a new heaven and a new earth, for the first heaven and the first earth had passed away, and there was no longer any sea. I saw the Holy City, the new Jerusalem, coming down out of heaven from God, prepared as a bride beautifully dressed for her husband. And I heard a loud voice from the throne saying, 'Look! God's dwelling place is now among the people, and He will dwell with them. They will be His people, and God Himself will be with them and be their God. He will wipe every tear from their eyes. There will be no more death, or mourning or crying or pain, for the old order of things has passed away."

"He who was seated on the throne said, "I am making everything new!" Then He said, "Write this down, for these words are trustworthy and true."

"He said to me: "It is done. I am the Alpha and the Omega, the Beginning and the End. To the thirsty I will give water without cost from the spring of the water of life. Those who are victorious will inherit all this, and I will be their God and they will be My children."

Revelation 22:12
"Behold, I am coming soon! My reward is with Me, and I will give to everyone according to what he has done." {Jesus}

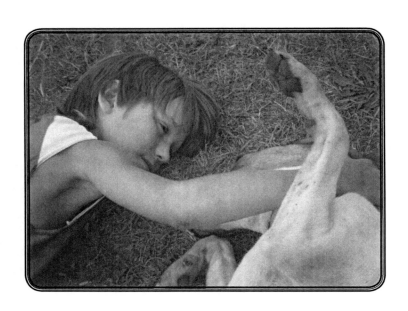

Being Where You Are

Chapter 8

There is a time for everything,
and a season for every activity under heaven;
a time to be born and a time to die,
. . .
a time to weep and a time to laugh,
a time to mourn and a time to dance,
. . .
a time to be silent and a time to speak
. . .

Ecclesiastes 3:1-8

Five steps of grief. Seven steps of grief. Twelve steps of grief.

I wanted to make sure that I stepped every one of them, so I read some books and did an Internet search to make sure that I was doing everything the experts said I should be doing when they said I should be doing them.

Denial? Hmm . . . No, I really do know that Trent is gone and I really do acknowledge it as God's perfect plan in my life granted from my loving Heavenly Father, just like Scripture says. I checked all the closets; he's not hiding in any of them.

Anger? Not yet. I hear it sometimes does come years down the road. Again, I remind myself that God is sovereign and He doesn't make any mistakes. Maybe I should ask my husband, but I don't think I've experienced the anger step yet.

Depression? I had to go through the list to see if I was on that step: overwhelming feelings of hopelessness, frustration, bitterness, self pity, mourning the loss of a person and the hopes, dreams, and plans for the future? Feeling lack of control, feeling numb? Perhaps feeling suicidal?

No, not really depressed, because again I know this was the perfect plan from my Heavenly Father. Suicidal? Only to the point that I am praying that God will hurry up and use me so that I, too, can go to heaven.

Acceptance? Can that really come before you have experienced all of the other emotions? The steps don't say that I can be there yet.

I guess I wouldn't be a good candidate for their little tests because I would fail miserably and skew all of their statistics. I went back to the whole trusting in God concept and figured that it would just be easier to take grief one day at a time, one moment at a time, one feeling at a time and combat it all with Scripture and prayer.

Shortly after the accident, God clearly revealed to me that others would struggle with what He was going to do with Trent's life, and with our family's response to it, but also that it was okay to let them struggle. I needed to be where God had me, not where He had them. God is big enough to handle all of our struggles, and often times those struggles are exactly what it takes to lead us closer to Him.

If anything, I am a people-pleaser to the core. It is a deep genetic trait that I blame on my mother and have passed along to my daughter. Smile, everything is perfectly fine; no, no, don't worry about me, I'm fine. In my quest to determine to walk this road as a God-pleaser, I have fought hard to overcome this engrained response.

My plea to my Heavenly Father became: "Where do you have me, Lord? Let me not be swayed by where others want me to be. Is it okay to rejoice when others are crying? Is it okay to be happy when others are sad? Isn't it just okay to trust You and believe every word You said in the Bible? Who am I really trying to please?"

From the very start I have determined to go straight through this process. Grief is a monster that haunts you until it is dealt with, one way or another. Head on is the best tactic that I have found.

I remember the morning after Trent died there was a big snowstorm with strong winds that blew the snow drifts four feet high in places. I put on my snow gear and intentionally headed for the biggest drift. I barreled straight through it, feeling the sinking of my boots, the struggle to lift them out again, the physical muscles it took to make it through that physical trial. Then I headed to the next big snow drift and tackled it as well. As every wave of grief comes at me, I can imagine that snow bank: one step at a time.

Grief will be patient with you. You can pretend that it doesn't affect you, but it will track you down years later and taunt you again until you deal with it. If it hurts, let it hurt. Feel every raw nerve of the pain. If it makes you happy, be happy. If you want to laugh, laugh. Smile on the good days. If you can't smile and the tears won't stop, just cry them out. If you are a screamer, scream. If you need to vent, vent. If you are a writer, write a book.

Release it. Feel it. Do it. Do it now, though, not later. It's okay to be right where you are. It's also okay if being right where you are takes ten minutes or ten days or ten weeks or even ten years. Allow God to lead. Follow Him. Trust Him. Every little detail is a weaving of God's perfect plan in your life. I am not the Master Designer who can fully explain to you why this life has to include pain and loss, but one day the Master Designer will explain it Himself to His children (1 Corinthians 13:12). The pain and the despair will only go as far as is necessary by your Heavenly Father who loves you. All He asks is that you trust Him in it.

The first few days, even weeks, after the accident were filled with wonderful people who loved us. Nonstop visitors, phone calls, e-mails, and a mailbox continuously full of sympathy cards. The days were filled with decisions and details and meetings and a funeral to plan and attend. In those earliest days after a loss there is a lot of adrenaline to keep a person going, but eventually you get tired.

It is so important to take the time to rest, eat well, and take care of yourself as you grieve. I am a hostess at heart and love having people in our home, but there came a time when I simply walked out of a kitchen full of family and friends, headed up the stairs, shut myself in my room, and crawled into bed. A good friend made it her mission to ensure that I was eating and drinking in the midst of the chaos and only ignored my reasoning that man does not live on bread alone (Matthew 4:4). She knew that I needed to take care of my physical needs so that it would be easier to fight the emotional and spiritual battles.

Rob and I tried to accept every person who came through our door as a person specifically sent by God. And most of those people brought some type of hamburger and tomato casserole or a huge package of toilet paper. This was especially a blessing, because I could hardly decide what to make for supper for the next two months let alone put together a hot dish or decide on which brand of toilet paper I should buy. It was very humbling to accept these gifts from our neighbors, friends, family and even strangers.

People went so far as to take our van in and get those grinding brakes fixed, a big crew of men and their sons did the majority of the remaining work to get the goat barn ready for the upcoming delivery time, and our dwindling stack of firewood was replenished.

At first we denied these gifts, but then we realized that they were God's provision for us in our time of need and that if we denied them we were actually stealing rewards from those who were called to give them. For those first few weeks we literally just stood back and watched God work through the exact people that He had called, and we praised Him for sending them.

Rest. Eat. Sleep. It's okay to let others do what God calls them to do for you. As a woman, especially, you need to let it go. Let them honor God by serving you for a little bit, and let them love you how they are called to love you. Let them come and fold your underwear and sweep your floors. Let them buy you pizza for supper and take your children for a while. If they ask what they can do, tell them. People want to love you and express that love in some tangible way, so let them. Feel the blessings of allowing them to love you.

In the midst of those busy days, find a place to grieve. Make a time to grieve. Hide if you need to, get away if you need to, shut the phone off and lock the doors if you need to.

One of the best things we did for our family, without even realizing it, was to take the trip to release Trent's ashes. The time away allowed the six of us to be together for several days straight where the majority of the people we saw did not know that our son and brother had just died. There were no questions to answer and no sympathetic looks directed our way. We could just be together and allow ourselves a break.

When the busyness and the drama ends, real life begins. Now what do you do? Everywhere I looked I saw Trent. His clothes in the hamper often sent me into crying fits, his school books were sitting on his desk never to be finished, and I could not look out the window without envisioning him roaming the woods. So, I did what I knew how to do—I resorted to physical work as it is often easier than emotional work. I cleaned closets and spare rooms and toilets and floors and barn stalls. I rearranged furniture and removed box after box and bag after bag of anything that wasn't nailed down in or around the house. And after I had worn myself out, Trent was still in heaven.

Foggy brain stage. Three words, but oh-so-hard to comprehend them. "What did you say? Umm, let me think about it, do I want pepperoni or sausage pizza?" Somewhere shortly after the funeral preparations, the actual funeral, all the visitors and writing out thank you cards, your brain will give out on you. That brain that you could count on to multitask as wife, mother, home school teacher, accountant, goat farmer, chief cook, bottle washer, and laundress will all of a sudden hit overload. Whoa! Stop the ride, Nellie! What was my name again?

There will literally be days, weeks, and even months, that you walk around in, well, a daze. The mental process that it will take to remember simple things like your phone number, what's for supper, and when the mortgage is due will take most of your effort. Those little things in life won't matter as much as the day before your loved one died, but somehow they still have to be done.

I am not a crier, but soon days followed that I could do nothing but cry. So I cried. I cried my sobbing, heart-aching tears in private. I cried on friends' shoulders. I cried with my kids. I cried with my husband. I watched my husband cry and it about broke my heart. So I cried some more.

The happy days can be just as hard as the crying days, though. At first I was filled with guilt when I was happy about something. Trent was not here, how could I ever be happy again? Finding pleasure in simple things without him was hard because, deep down, did that then mean that I was happy when my son was dead?

Again, I had to go back to the promises of Scripture and remind myself of the things that I knew to be true. God is sovereign and this was His perfect plan. God said that His grace is sufficient, and that His power is made perfect in my weakness (2 Corinthians 12:9). God has called His children to rejoice even in the midst of grief because of our hope that is found in Jesus (1 Peter 1: 3-9). My living does not bring my son back. My living only proves that I trust God for leaving me here at this time.

Your loss is real. Your pain is real. Don't deny it. Don't go numb. Don't pretend it away. Face it and go straight through it. God is leading you and promises that He will never let you go.

Rob struggled to go back to work even with a month off after the accident. When your life has just been turned upside down, and death is real in your world, it is hard to watch everybody else simply living their normal lives. Besides not being able to think clearly, he had eternity weighing heavily on his heart. It's so difficult after a loved one's death to look around and see very few people with any concern of eternity, even their own eternity.

Others will soon forget about your loss. Their life will go on and they will still have their children. Most people won't know what to say to you in just a short amount of time. Everybody hugs you and asks how you're doing at the beginning, but pretty soon nobody knows what to say, so they don't say anything at all. They don't want to make you cry and they don't know if they should bring up the subject or not, so they don't. The proverbial big white elephant is standing on both of your toes and you talk about the weather.

In a little community, the grocery store was one of my worst fears. What if I break down and cry over deciding how many pounds of bananas to buy? What if the checkout lady asks how I'm doing today and I actually tell her and she starts crying? The people who really don't know you, but have been talking about you since the accident and have been too scared to talk to you, turn and walk away and pretend that they didn't see you. I did a lot of shopping at big stores in different towns the first few months after the accident.

Those same people who won't say anything will be replaced with the people who say—excuse me—stupid things. Forgive them; give them much grace, run away from them if you have to. You do not have to explain to everybody about how your loved one died. I have had strangers want to know every detail about Trent's death. "Was it a tree, was it a boulder, did he hit his head or his chest?" they wanted to know. I referred them back to Jesus and their own eternity. That usually makes them change the subject very quickly.

Fear is a part of grief. Especially at night when it's too quiet and sleep won't come, or sleep does come and along with it come the dreams: skis or skates and hills and looking for who died. Clinging to your husband to make sure that he is really still there. Squeezing your eyes shut tight so that at least you can pretend you might fall back to sleep. But God is there, too. His hand is still holding you and His work is still being done. Hold on tighter. God really does know what He's doing.

Shortly after Trent died the thought came to both Rob and I that there were still no guarantees that we would never lose another child. Nowhere in Scripture does it say that once you've lost one child God won't take any others. We willingly offered our other children up to God, begging Him for their salvation first, but surrendering any hold we ever thought we had on any part of the children's lives with whom He had entrusted us.

I entertained anger for about two minutes. Then I remembered my Savior and how He responded to God's calling for His earthly time here. He accepted God's plan and wasn't angry about it. Rather than giving in to this required step, I have resolved to allow myself to follow Jesus' example and accept God's will in my life as well, without anger.

You need to deal with God and reconcile what He has chosen to do in His sovereignty. For us it was easy to call it good and rejoice with Him in the midst of Trent's death, even through the pain and the tears. Our prayers for Trent's salvation and his dwelling in heaven forever had been answered. We knew that Trent was safe while the rest of our children were still in the "enemy territory". Trent was no longer enslaved here by sin, weighed down by the oppressor, but rather he was free. He was in the presence of God. He was standing before the throne worshiping his Savior. It was not for him that we cried, but for ourselves and how much we would miss him until we were called home to heaven.

After the first few weeks of rejoicing that Trent was in heaven, I started to be overwhelmed with where he was. I missed him intensely and could not imagine where he was at that very moment or what he was doing. This boy who had sat at my supper table just the night before the accident, the boy who always wanted to race on our way up from the barn, the boy who always wanted a kiss goodnight—where was he now? I had said for years that I trusted God for His plans and I have heard about heaven my whole life, but now I had to live those words. A certain anxiety of not being able to go get him and bring him home, like when he was at camp or at a friend's house, overwhelmed me.

We can set things aside for only so long as we retrain our brain and our thoughts, but eventually our mind always wants to come back to what it knows. For nearly thirteen years I knew Trent to be here. Now he wasn't here. My soul knew that he was in heaven, but my brain wanted to know where he was so that

I could rationalize his absence on an earthly level. All I could do was trust God in this as well.

Trusting God is sometimes simply that, just trusting Him. Without seeing Him, without knowing His plans, without knowing the why's, or the who's, or the how's. Total trust. It means not having to know the little details today. It means longing all the more for God's kingdom to come so that one day we will know first hand. It means letting God be God in how He does things, which often times means not knowing all the "why's", but just letting Him take our hand and lead us where He wants us to go.

Can it be enough to wait until we get to heaven to receive the answers? Can it be enough that God will make sense of it all on the other side of this life? Can't we just trust Him?

We may not have all the small answers, but God has clearly given us the big answers in His Word. Does He love His children? Yes (John 3:16). Does He only do things in our lives that work for our good? Yes (Romans 8:28). Does He promise to be faithful, never to leave us or forsake us? Yes (Hebrews 13:5). Has He promised to walk with us the whole way until we see Him face to face? Yes (Psalm 139:7-16). Hasn't He promised rewards for those who are faithful? Yes (Revelation 22:12). If we can trust Him for the big things, then we can certainly trust Him for the small things.

The "firsts" after the accident were very hard. The first Monday without Trent, the first grocery shopping trip without Trent, the first birthday without Trent, the first trip to camp without Trent. There are so many firsts. And they all hurt. They all remind you of your loss again and again. Even in light of sharing in the joy of God working His glorious plan through your loss you still face the hurt of those "firsts".

I recall lamenting along with Jonah in chapter 4 as he sat under that leafy plant that grew up for shade. Lamenting in "Why me? Why death? Why my son? Why this way?" I couldn't understand what I couldn't see, and I longed for my son. I soon realized that Trent was not missing out on anything here on this earth, it was me who was missing out on having him here.

Missing your loved one does not mean that you aren't trusting God. The pain of missing somebody is an agonizing pain that runs deep through your soul. This person that you loved and knew intimately on this earth is now no longer a part of your life here, and there is nothing that you can do about it. Your Heavenly Father knows your pain. He feels your pain and offers to be enough if you will let Him. Will you let Him?

Take time to praise God. My overwhelming thought after Trent's accident was to praise God that He had saved Trent. Above all else, overshadowing the pain and the loss, I could praise God for Trent's salvation. In the darkest moments there was still the pinhole of light and hope: I knew that my son was in heaven. The morning after the accident I woke up with prayers of praise on my lips that Trent was in heaven, and it has become a habit that I have continued everyday since to prepare myself for the day ahead and whatever God has in store.

Rest in God's promises: this is His work. He who began a good work in you will finish it to the end (Philippians 1:6). He who called you to this trial is faithful. You only have to grieve one day at a time, so don't worry about tomorrow, it has enough worries of it's own (Matthew 6:34). Live today and be where God has you today.

As a Christian, be sure to surround yourself with other believers. God graciously provided people who were faithful in praying for our family, and who were also faithful in letting us know that they were praying. Friends and family, and even people that we have never met, were brought into our lives at this time to lift us up before the throne of God so that we could endure this high calling in our lives.

Make yourself accountable in some way to let others know how you're doing and how they can pray for you. Tell them what you need and also when you need encouragement. Don't assume they know; tell them. You are not being selfish to ask others to pick you up, and to hold you up, during this difficult time.

Give yourself an outlet. Somehow your grief has to be expressed. Only you know how you can do that. If you keep it all inside you will one day explode in some way that will only hurt you and others. Your grief needs to be let out, so find a way to release it. Glorify God in the releasing of it.

My outlet is writing. When I write I no longer carry those thoughts inside of me. I watch God move and work through words on a computer screen. Those words release my brain from carrying the overwhelming thoughts and emotions that quickly become a burden. They allow what God is doing in my life to take a form, and more importantly, they force me to look at them and make sure that they line up with Scripture. Through writing I can lay down my fears and worries and leave them at the foot of the cross.

Jesus said that His yoke is easy and His burden is light (Matthew 11:28-30). If you are trying to carry a yoke that is too heavy, simply give it back to Jesus. He has only called you to abide in Him and trust Him. Let Him carry what He needs to carry.

As the battle continues, I fight to remind myself of what Paul says in Philippians 1:23: "It is better to be in the presence of Christ than to go on living here in this world." Even for my son. Trent is in the presence of the living God. What could compare here on this earth? For what would I wish him back if it meant taking him from his Savior?

Just give yourself some time. Don't rush through grief. Wait before making any major life changes like selling the farm or starting another adoption. Let the dust settle. Those things will come when God calls you to them. Don't escape grief by causing chaos in your life. Deal with this pain of loss and then move on to the next good works when God calls you to move on. Be right where He has you right now.

There are days that I see Trent everywhere, and then there are days that I can't see him anywhere. My brain struggles to remember every little detail about him: his smile, his giggle, his eyes, what color his toothbrush was, what it felt like to hold him in my arms. On those days I remind myself that eternity is a very long time, and though I long for my son here and now, I will have him then and death can never take him again.

The Good Works Left for You to Do

Chapter 9

For we are God's workmanship,
created in Christ Jesus to do good works,
which God prepared in advance for us to do.

Ephesians 2:10

God took Trent, not me.

That simple revelation was one of the first things that God made clear to me the morning after Trent's accident. The words from Ephesians 2:10 rang through my mind reminding me again that God had good works prepared in advance specifically for me to do, just like He had His good works prepared in advance for Trent to do. Trent's days of doing those good works on earth were finished. But maybe the good works prepared for Trent's life would be greater fulfilled through his death. Maybe Trent's death was just the beginning of the ripple effect of God's good works that were now being veiled by our pain.

God made me a worker to the core. In His sovereignty, God ordained that there would be six goats on our little farm scheduled to give birth beginning just two days after Trent's funeral. It certainly gave me a reason to get out of bed in the mornings following the accident. The physical work of farming and taking care of my family gave me tangible things to do to keep busy.

But after Trent died I longed all the more for God's work. I saw the fleeting days of my life in this world and had just seen firsthand how none of this world's treasures will go with us into eternity. Along with Rob, I felt the immense weight of unsaved souls all around me. I understood on a deeper level my own apathy towards those souls, which caused me to refrain from even sharing the gospel with them. The things in my life that used to matter faded in the distance when compared to eternity.

God filled both Rob and myself with a longing for heaven, as well as an eagerness to tell others about Jesus and His salvation. What else really matters? All of Trent's belongings are still here. His guns, his socks, his prized possessions and trophies are all lying on his bed waiting to get packed up and stored away or sent to the Goodwill. Again, what else really matters?

Was Scripture right when it said that we will gladly throw all of these earthly belongings to the rodents and bats (Isaiah 2:20) when we see what Christ offers His children? Why then had we been wasting so much time pursuing the things of this world?

Our prayer and our plea became that if God was going to keep us here He would bring us mighty works to do to advance His kingdom. I can bravely face every day because I realize that God has the day of my death ordained as well. As long as I am here I can trust that it is because God's good works for my life that will bring glory to His name are not yet finished. I long to be used by Him all the more.

Beginning at the funeral, God called Rob to speak publicly about Trent's short life and to present the gospel message. But God not only called Rob, He equipped him as well. My husband, who rarely shares in the conversation at the dinner table, was boldly proclaiming the Word of God from pulpits and lawns, on stages, and in church basements and camp chapels to many who needed to see and hear the reality of eternity. The passion and desire that God gave Rob to share the gospel has encouraged me greatly, and many other lives as well. No telemarketer or Menard's salesman was safe from this man with the passion to share the good news of salvation.

It is so easy to think that because God has called one person one way that you yourself should be doing the same work. For myself, I could hardly utter three words to finish a complete sentence that made any sense in the weeks after the accident, but I could write. So I wrote and Rob talked, both of us telling the same story: the message of a young boy's life that God chose to use to reveal salvation to many, the message of eternity appearing before we expected it, the message of the good news of a Savior that came to redeem His children and to offer forgiveness for those who would accept it.

When a family is grieving it is especially important to encourage children to live the life God gave them to live. As much as I felt that God had called me to continue to live, I felt the need for my children to be able to live all the more. I have struggled hard to balance helping them grieve the depth of the pain of losing their brother without making it their own death. I do not want their childhood, and the rest of their lives, to be about the day their brother died. God made each of them with their own lives to live and their own good works to do.

It amazed me to watch the children who were affected by Trent's death. The day after the accident, when the house was overflowing and the multitude of kids were all enjoying the party, one of my sister's six children came and told their mom they couldn't find Trent. Traci explained to them again that

Trent had died and was in heaven, remember? Oh that's right, and off they went to play again. Their childlike faith reminded me to trust God all the more.

Grief does affect children, though, and we have been careful to watch our kids closely and be aware of how each child struggles differently. We have one child who is very blunt and expresses emotion in a very painful way. It was not uncommon to hear hurtful comments in the days that followed Trent's accident. Another child doesn't express feelings openly, and yet another child overtly cries and laments over the loss, fully trusting God but missing Trent immensely. Another child saw clearly the distinction between heaven and hell and longs for heaven because of Trent's death.

A simple hug when the sorrow is too great, a bedtime talk, a quiet prayer, a candlelit bath, painting each others toenails, and even milking goats together have become ways to share our grief and minister to each other. All of these little things are grande works in our Heavenly Father's kingdom because they bring a peace and redirecting as we care for one another. These simple acts of kindness allow us to be the hands and feet of Christ as we reflect His love in simple ways.

We soon realized that we, as a family, were not the only ones grieving. The loss felt by those around us who also loved Trent, and the grief that they were experiencing, was just as real as ours. Grandmothers and aunts and uncles, cousins and neighbors and friends, and even the library ladies and the checkout girl at the local Family Dollar store were all struck with our tragedy.

What I had to realize, as well, was that I couldn't "fix" that pain for them. But I could acknowledge it. I could let them know that it was okay if they cried, too. I could love them and hold them while they grieved. I could point them to Jesus and His promises.

This was their grandson, their nephew, their friend. Their lives will also be forever changed because of that day. They needed to know that they were allowed to grieve deeply as well, even if it wasn't their son who had died. Their pain was just as real as ours. The work that God was doing in their lives was just as real, too.

In the seventeenth chapter of John, Jesus is praying for Himself, for His disciples, and for all those that God had given Him out of the world. Jesus' time here on this earth, as well as His work, was close to being finished. His ultimate desire was that God would be glorified, and that His glory would be seen through the completion of the work that God had given Him to do.

Has God not also called each of us, as His children, to a specific purpose in this life to do good works that will glorify His name? When those good works are done, and in His perfect timing, He will call us home, too.

What has God called you to in your own time of suffering? Will you let God use you in this master plan of His? Will you accept His ways and glorify His name in it as Scripture lays out? Will you humbly bow and acknowledge Him as Lord of your life? Will you willingly follow where He leads?

Especially as a grieving Christian, you are now in the spotlight, like it or not. Your theology and your understanding of God are revealed, both to yourself and to your world of watchers. Do you really believe that what He is doing is for your good? Do you believe that His ways are better than yours? There is such freedom in letting God lead and simply trusting Him to be God.

Rob and I are striving to run the race of our lives well while in pursuit of the great prize promised in Scripture (Hebrews 12:1-2). As odd as it sounds, we are grateful that God woke us up through this tragedy so that we can see beyond this world and not waste our remaining time here. If only what is done for Christ will last, then we will strain all the harder to do the good works prepared in advance for His glory.

The words that my Dad told me twenty years ago continue to echo through my life: "Terri, there is nothing more important than God." How true those words still are, Dad, how true they are.

But You're Doing It

Chapter 10

*God has said "Never will I leave you;
Never will I forsake you."*

Hebrews 13:5b

There is no right or wrong way to grieve. What matters is that you do it.

Grief is not something that we choose for ourselves, but rather it is a position that we are thrust into. There is usually little preparation and nobody asked if you wanted to have your child taken from you.

As difficult as it is to realize, the world does not stop because your loved one has died. Grief doesn't take a break, but life won't allow you stay on the couch in the fetal position for very long. The brakes on the van will still need to be fixed, the floors will still need to be swept, and somebody will eventually drink the last glass of milk. Never do you stop missing your loved one, but life continues to go on, as unfair as that may seem.

But how do you go on living? How do you find purpose in this life again?

I wish I had the answer for you. A quick checklist that would instantly allow you to jump through this hoop of grief and get you back on that other side where life is "normal" again.

There is a new normal now. Not a normal that you will want to easily accept or one that is without pain, but one that needs to be embraced.

You need to find a reason to keep getting out of bed in the morning and to live. Live for your spouse. Live for your children. Live for your dog. Live because the coffee is hot and the sun still comes up everyday. Live for yourself. Live because God still has you here with good works for you to do for His kingdom. Find a reason, and then live.

Everyday that you go forth in the hope of Christ you are doing it. You are living. His grace really is sufficient; His mercies are new each morning; He will be faithful this day as well (2 Corinthians 12:9; Lamentations 3:22-23; 1 Corinthians 1:9). I can't promise you that it get's any easier, or that the pain will dull with time. What I can promise you is that God knows exactly what He's doing.

You can trust Him, even in the pain, even in the despair, even in the tears, even in the smiles, and even in the times of joy. Be where He has you. Feel Him wrap His loving arms around you as you cry. He says that He is bottling up every one of your tears (Psalm 56:8 ESV).

Hold on to His hand as He leads. The way may be scary and the heartache will hurt, the pit may be deep and dark and ugly, but hold on tight. When this world is over, dear Christian, He promises to make everything right, even this time of suffering.

Keep grieving, keep living, keep feeling, keep looking up because Jesus who is faithful is coming soon and His reward is with Him. He promised.

What if it Had Been You?

Chapter 11

Here I am!
I stand at the door and knock.
If anyone hears my voice and opens the door,
I will come in.

Revelation 3:20a

Salvation has never meant more than at this time in my life.

Trent's salvation has never been more important. My own salvation, and the salvation of my husband, children and loved ones have never weighed heavier on my heart.

Eternity is a long time. Where will you spend it, dear reader? Do you know this Savior of mine? His name is Jesus. He said that He would forgive every sin that you have ever committed. He offers peace that is overflowing, blessings for obedience, and best of all eternity with Him in Heaven.

But His requirements are high. It will cost you your life.

He said that we must first confess with our mouths that we are sinners (Romans 10:9). Do you know what sin is? Sin is anything that does not bring glory to God: every word, every thought, every action we do, or do not do, that does not glorify God. He alone is perfect and holy and worthy to be praised and to receive honor and glory (Revelation 4:11).

God's standards are so high that He considers lust to be adultery (Matthew 5:27-28). He considers hatred to be murder (Matthew 5:21-22). The Bible says that all have sinned and have fallen short of the glory of God (Romans 3:23). That includes you and me. Our offenses against God's glory are so atrocious that an eternity in Hell is the only just punishment for them (2 Thessalonians 1:8-9). Do you know that you are a sinner? Have you acknowledged your own sinfulness before God?

But those who call on the name of the Lord Jesus will be saved (Romans 10:13).

God graciously provided His perfect Son, Jesus Christ, as the atonement for our sins through His death on the cross. What God requires is that we simply believe in our hearts and confess with our mouths that Jesus died in our place to pay the penalty for our sinfulness. There is nothing that we can do to earn our salvation, but rather, we must acknowledge God alone for His free gift. The Holy Spirit's work of sanctification in our life, which causes repentance of our sins, is proof of that salvation as we watch our desires change to longing to please God rather than our sinful nature.

So let me ask you what we have asked so many others: "What if it had been you that died in that skiing accident? Where would you be right now?"

What are you counting on to spend eternity in Heaven? Are you trying to attain salvation by your own works? Are you adding Jesus plus your presumed goodness, your faithfulness, your deeds? Are you still trying to clean up your life first before you come to the Father for forgiveness? What will you say when He asks you why He should let you into His Heaven? Are you willing to accept His offer for salvation?

Scripture says that it is only through the blood of Jesus that you will enter.

Enter through the narrow gate. For wide is the gate and broad is the road that leads to destruction, and many enter through it. But small is the gate and narrow the road that leads to life, and only a few find it (Matthew 7:13-14).

My prayer is that you know my Savior, Jesus Christ, and are willing to trust Him wherever He may lead you.

The Romans Road to Salvation:

For all have sinned and fall short of the Glory of God.

As it is written:

There is no one righteous, not even one; there is no one who understands, no one who seeks God. All have turned away, they have together become worthless; there is no one who does good, not even one. Their mouths are open graves; their tongues practice deceit. The poison of vipers is on their lips. Their mouths are full of cursing and bitterness. Their feet are swift to shed blood; ruin and misery mark their ways, and the way of peace they do not know. There is no fear of God before their eyes.

For the wages of sin is death, but the gift of God is eternal life in Christ Jesus our Lord.

God demonstrated His own love for us in this: While we were still sinners, Christ died for us.

If you confess with your mouth, "Jesus is Lord," and believe in your heart that God raised Him from the dead, you will be saved.

For everyone who calls on the name of the Lord will be saved.

Therefore, since we have been justified through faith, we have peace with God through our Lord Jesus Christ.

There is now no condemnation for those who are in Christ Jesus.

For I am convinced that neither death nor life, neither angels nor demons, neither the present nor the future, nor any powers, neither height nor depth, nor anything else in all creation, will be able to separate us from the love of God that is in Christ Jesus our Lord.

Jesus replied, "If anyone loves me, he will obey my teaching."

Romans 3:23; 3:10-18; 6:23; 5:8; 10:9; 10:13; 5:1; 8:1; 8:38-39; John 14:23a

Part 3

The Blog Posts

The Way It Was

Chapter 12

~~✦~~

"You are my witnesses,"
declares the Lord,
"that I am God."

Isaiah 43:12b

In the summer of 2008 Trent encouraged me to start a blog.

He always took credit that he was the instigator and the reason that Mom took so many pictures. Little did I know back then how God would use that blog in our lives, and especially with Trent's life. It has become a treasure trove of family photos, a gathering place for new and old friends, a keeper of records and details of a time when life was "normal". And more than that, it has been a way to watch God weave His sovereignty in the plans He has for our lives.

The following are some edited blog posts from before and after Trent's accident sharing the raw moment-to-moment journey of walking with Jesus. You can read more at: HowMySaviorLeadsMe.blogspot.com

God Stuff

May 18, 2010

The days are going by so fast. It seems that I don't take time out to really stop and see what God has been doing in my life and heart, and also in the lives He has chosen to put around me. In my quiet time this morning I was pondering so many things of the last few weeks, and it made me rejoice in my Lord all over again. It is easy to be discouraged, but when we really start counting our blessings it puts our hearts right.

Some of my bigger God moments from the past few days:

I love how God takes my broken, sinful nature and somehow has used that to nurture these five beautiful children with whom He has entrusted me for all these years. To see one certain young man (Trent) repent and become right with God has caused me to be in total awe. Another certain daughter has so surpassed me both in her love for her Lord and her knowledge and desire to know Him more that I can only sit back and wonder what God will do with the rest of her young life. A husband who holds so strongly to the Lord and His Word has been my steady rock for so many ups and downs.

I love how God is so gracious in my disobedience. Rather than giving me what I deserve, He wraps His arms around me in my disgruntled state and leads me ever so gently to His word. Unmistakably, He leads me to the very Scripture passage He ordained to be written hundreds of years ago so that He might whisper it into my ear now and bring repentance. And when I put my feelings before His words, He forgives even that.

I love watching how God puts people right smack in the middle of my life when I'm not even aware of it, and then takes such persons and allows me to watch Him transform them. How He grows me right alongside them and allows them to watch the growth in me as well. There is nothing like getting to rejoice in their joys, and wrap my arms around them in their repentance.

I love how God reunites people after hurt and allows rejoicing in the works of His hand. When His time has finally come to bring things to completion and together we can anticipate what He will do next.

I love how God used His Son Jesus to remove the sting of death, even from a too-young-mother's early homecoming. How, somehow, in the midst of cancer and death a family can rejoice that she is now with her Savior and long for their own meeting with their Maker.

I love it when God uses something as simple as a few quiet moments and lots of questions in the midst of a 30-hour weekend shift to share the gospel with a friend who He has continued to bring into every area of my life. I love it even more when He gives me the words to say.

I love knowing that therefore, there is now no condemnation for those who are in Christ Jesus. That for an eternity I will keep learning how wide, and how long, and how high, and how deep is the love of Christ for me (Romans 8:1, Ephesians 3:18).

Again I Say Rejoice!

January 23, 2011

Finally, my brothers, rejoice in the Lord! Philippians 3:1

*

Rejoice: To feel joyful; to delight in.

*

This verse is bound to become my favorite verse of the year for 2011. What a few simple words, yet so much depth, and so applicable to everything in life. It puts a lot of things into perspective. Rejoice, Paul says! Rejoice in God being sovereign over every little detail! Rejoice in my salvation! Rejoice in God allowing me to be here among critters and husband and kids and woods and wide-open spaces and half finished barns! Rejoice in His plans rather than my own! Rejoice in revelations! Rejoice in the Word! Rejoice in plenty and in want! Rejoice in too much work! Rejoice in old, cold farmhouses! Rejoice in the Lord always! I will say it again: Rejoice!

Ouch!

February 1, 2011

*   *   *

*I rise before dawn and cry for help; I have put my
hope in your word. Psalm 119:147*

*   *   *

I am no stranger to pain, but the last day or so has brought the intensity of it up just a notch higher. For several years we have fed our animals with round bales. Hay rings for the bigger ones, but for the goats we peel the layers of hay off twice a day. And, about this time every year, I have felt the daily wear and tear that the work has on my back. Not one to grumble much (out loud at least) or expect others to help (a bit of pride perhaps) I keep going. But add into that a silly horse with one too many trips of bouncy trotting and quick, spinning turns to head back home, and I was really feeling it last week. I iced it and took the weekend off from riding (to sit at an ER desk). It felt much better until yesterday, with the sun shining, temps around 10 and itching to ride Russell's trails again, the girls and I headed out on our mighty steeds. All was well until about halfway through the woods when, in the midst of a sudden, unexpected, quick, spinning turn to head back home, something in my back was re-jolted. Ouch! I had no choice but to make it back home (mostly on top of my horse) and figured everything would be fine with a bit of ibuprofen, ice, heat, and a massage. But the pain has only worsened and I am even considering actually heading into the dreaded doctor's office today.

* * *

It was good for me to be afflicted, so that I might
learn your decrees. Psalm 119:71

* * *

Finally getting out of bed due to the pain around 5:00 a.m. has turned into a good thing, though. It is rare alone-time to ponder God and life and love. Precious, quiet moments to think and pray before the kids or the dogs are up. Time to be in Scripture and savor the Word of God. I have been learning to trust God more and more and in a different way over the past couple of years. Learning the cost of standing on His Word, seeing my own desires being stronger than wanting to stand on His Word, and then seeing Him still love me and grow me despite it. The sweet words expressed in Psalm 119 could have been mine this morning as I read the Psalmist's plea to God to do something about the sin and corruptness that he saw all around, the sin and corruptness in the world, in the church, in his heart, in my own heart. Repenting of my own ways and clinging to the laws, hopes and promises found in Scripture. Trusting and waiting until the day that God will be faithful to them.

* * *

Accept, O Lord, the willing praise of my mouth,
and teach me your laws. Psalm 119:108

* * *

Time in the recliner has also given me the opportunity to read one of my favorite books, *The God I Love* by Joni

Eareckson Tada. You see, I believe what Scripture teaches about God's sovereignty. That everything, every situation, every joy, every hardship, every decision is ordained by God and is for His glory, yet somehow in that we are still responsible for our decisions, our sin, our actions. I don't pretend to understand how it all works together, but there is great peace in knowing that God has it all worked out for our joy and His glory. Knowing that for some reason my intense pain is in His plan for good, to know that all the hard stuff and the "junk" is being used for transforming me to look more like Christ. The kids and I were reading in Judges 1-5 yesterday and found it interesting that God allowed hardships to be left in the Israelite's lives to allow them the struggle to choose to serve Him. It made me ponder all the "struggles" I can find to whine about in my life and decide if I am going to choose to see them as ways to glorify God or use them as stumbling blocks for my own destruction.

* * *

. . . but I will ponder your statutes. Psalm 119:95b

* * *

Joni Eareckson Tada touches on her own struggle with this in her questioning's on the "whys" and "what-ifs" of God's plan for her life prior to the accident that would put her in a wheelchair for the rest of her life, leaving her dependent on others, but ultimately would lead her to knowing God in a deeper way than she ever would have known Him without it. Just weeks before she dived into the water, not realizing that she would soon never walk again, she sensed God's dissatisfaction over her mediocrity with Him. She felt challenged by God's divine dare of sorts, and the possibility of having to trust Him in a high calling for her life. It would force her to decide if she was really committed to following Jesus whatever the cost. Was she afraid? Could she do it?

* * *
My comfort in my suffering is this: Your promise
preserves my life. Psalm 119:50
* * *

The quote, coming on the tail-end of a conversation with Rob last night, really struck me because, first of all, I have been pretty mediocre with God as of late and have been able to justify it with being a tired mom, the cares of the world, children, work, husband, farm, and I really didn't need it pointed out thank-you-very-much. That and, yes, I am afraid. I mean, what if I had to take a stand for God, and {gasp} really trust Him? Loving the unlovable, putting down my stones, admitting failure, getting out of my comfort zone, allowing Him to love me, forgive me, heal me, use me. It would mean accepting His plans, letting go of my own. Can I follow Him? I don't know, God. Can I do it? Full surrender?

* * *
Let me understand the teachings of your precepts;
then I will meditate on your wonders.
Psalm 119:27
* * *

I think by nature we are a short-minded, short-sighted people. If we don't see the results in two minutes or less, we want our money back. Sometimes it seems too hard to ponder the deep things of God that take soul searching, sorting, and tough decisions. Is His Word truth? Will I live by it and trust it? Will I give up the world because He is greater? Is my sin really that bad? Is my time really that worthy (for Bible study, prayer, church, to invest in my children, etc.)? In my life I tend to always want a quick fix. I want God to come riding in on His white horse (without a sore back) and rescue me from whatever my latest affliction is. I don't want to endure eleven years of daily pain in order for His message to sink in that these bodies are not eternal and which causes heaven to look all the better. I don't want dividing lines in relationships over the word that cause strife. I don't want to stand alone. I don't want to suffer. Deep down, I really just want the cotton candy and the pony rides.

* * *

Accept, O Lord, the willing praise of my mouth,
and teach me your laws. Psalm 119:108

* * *

A quote from a long-ago pastor:

> If you are not growing in Holiness (*The state or quality of being holy; perfect moral integrity or purity; freedom from sin; sanctity; innocence*), you've never been justified (*to free from blame*). Justification always causes sanctification (*to make holy; set apart as sacred; consecrate; to purify or free from sin; to make productive of or conducive to spiritual blessing*).

So I guess I am somewhere in that sanctification process. Praising the Lord who died in my place to make it all possible. Trusting the One who ordained it. Waiting eagerly for the day He will reveal it, and finding joy in the midst of it.

A New Home

February 19, 2011

On Friday February 18th, 2011, our 12-year-old son, Trent, went home to heaven. God's peace that surpasses all understanding is at this point being poured out on our household and we are rejoicing in His goodness. God granted Trent salvation last summer and we all enjoyed the fruit in his

111

young life. Already we are seeing God move in mighty ways and desire to see Him glorified through this. Dance before your King, my son.

His Mercies are New Everyday

February 21, 2011

Thank you for sharing this walk with us friends! Know that God's plans and God's grace are greater than ours. We have been rejoicing since Friday for the good work that God has done! We have prayed for over twelve years for Trent to go to heaven, and to be used by God in a mighty way, and God has honored our petitions. Who are we to complain when and how? Trent died in a skiing accident while on a trip with his youth group in Duluth, MN. In God's sovereignty he went just the way he would have wanted to go: in the woods, instantly. God's mercies have been many and amazing! We are praising Him for them!

Sweet, Sweet Words

February 23, 2011

God is good! He has allowed us great rejoicing! We have seen Him move in mightier ways than we could have ever imagined. The details are becoming a bit overwhelming at this point, and coupled with very little sleep, no appetite, and ministering to all who walk through our door, we are getting tired. God will take care of those little details, and as long as

He gives us the strength and the clarity, we will press on. We will rest when He gives us that as well.

We were able to take a trip to buy new celebration clothes yesterday. As most of you all know I am very frugal, so this was a big part of our rejoicing and celebrating in preparation for tomorrow. The funeral plans are coming together: it's like planning a wedding for our son in less than a week. Numerous people have stepped in and blessed us, and I have actually allowed them to do so.

The details that God has given us to handle He has also been faithful to give us the strength to accomplish. We are being diligent to continue to find our strength only in the Lord and hold tightly to Scripture, prayer, and worship. As a family we are watching out closely for each other, and so far God has allowed us all to be like-minded as we long for God's glory to be revealed in all of this. What an honor to be a part of His work. God lead me to Philippians this morning and the promises found in there were oh-so sweet.

Just a few more of God's whispers to me over the past few days: This has been granted to me as a gift (Philippians 1:29). It is all right to rejoice over this good work of God forever (Isaiah 65:18). I can take Jesus as my example when He considered God's plan for salvation (Matthew 26:36-44). He accepted that it would be done through death, and he never got angry or questioned God, but rather submitted and praised Him for His wisdom. God's will be done, not mine. I am free to do the same and trust my heavenly Father in this as well. We can praise God for this, even if we watch others around us struggle with God through it.

This is the Day

February 24, 2011

This is the day that the Lord has made, and we are rejoicing in it. This is the day to celebrate Trent's short life here in this world and worship the God who has ordained the steps to bring him home to heaven. The anticipation in our house is so high right now as we look forward to being used, yet again, to be a witness and a testimony to the work and hope of God at the funeral/celebration service this afternoon. Please continue your prayers that God would work in a mighty way today, in both believers and non-believers. Already we are seeing the fruit of salvation that God promised would come from our afflictions. The gospel has gone forth just as He promised it would and we have seen the beginning of the elect that God will call through this.

Christians and non-Christians alike are baffled by what God is doing in our lives. We are smiling fools to many! God has granted us peace and joy in His plan. He has pried our fingers off of this world even more, and given us a heart for all the lost souls around us. He has made us bold. He has made us strong. He has made us to be full of rejoicing in His perfect plan. Our son is in heaven, how could we not rejoice if we believe what the Bible says?

Know that we are so grateful for the prayers that have been offered up on our behalf as we credit none of this to ourselves. God has placed each one of you in our lives to be the support that holds us up, just as Aaron and Hur held up Moses' arms that the battle would be won. This is a battle for souls—souls that will live forever in eternity. God has called so many to decide to choose this day whom they will serve. Choose today, because He may not let you have another opportunity to decide. We have prayed for the walls to be built high and thick around us as we boldly proclaim what God is doing. I can just imagine Trent in heaven right now as he watches God's work and rejoices with us.

The Morning After

February 25, 2011

Everybody has told me that it will be the day after the funeral and the weeks, months, and years after that will be hard. So, given this is the dreaded "morning after", I have found since last night that for their sake (because I tend to be a people-pleaser at my core) I think it is only appropriate to crash now. Since Friday I have determined to do only one thing at a time, to finish one detail before I move on to the next good work that God has ordained. His grace is sufficient for today, tomorrow has enough worries of it's own. We have watched God be with us and give us strength every step of the way so far, and we are determined to realize that it is only by His grace that we will take every other step as well for the rest of our lives.

My thoughts over the last couple of days, and especially this morning, have been about being refined by God's fire. When the day comes to write the whole story I will rejoice in the twenty years that God has been preparing me for this, but for now I need to remember His abundant mercy, love, tenderness, and promises that will sustain me until I enter glory. I am living so much more eternally minded because of what God did on Friday. Looking ahead to the day when all things will be tested by God's fire. What was built with precious gold and stone will be revealed, and what was built with hay and stubble will also be revealed (1 Corinthians 3:12-13).

Trent's life was precious gold and stone to his mother's heart. His loss will stand the fire just as Scripture has said, that the gospel will go forth with much sorrow and heartache. What I find myself being aware of right now is how I go about building the rest. Will I choose to believe what God has promised: that this is His good work, that He is sovereign, that He really does have every day planned, even Friday? Will I build this up to be a poor Terri pity party so that I get the glory? Or, with everything that is within me and with all the strength that God gives me, will I hold on to knowing and somehow extolling that this is all about God and Him being glorified? Will other's souls be of higher importance to me at this time?

I know that Trent is in heaven. I watched God work in his life. God has revealed and proven enough other Scripture passages to me that it is a simple equation in my brain to see that God did what Scripture says in how He saved Trent (He allowed us to see Trent's hard heart, revealing to us clearly that he was dead in sin. God then saved him, not by our coaxing at the time, etc., but clearly at a time that God had changed his heart), and I am confident that Trent is now in heaven.

So this "morning after" I have determined to be where God wants me, not where everybody else thinks I should be. I have begged God to never let me want Trent back here. There is nothing here that I would want him back for if it denies him being with God. I want to always praise God for His perfect plan of salvation. Those who love salvation love God's ways (Psalm 40).

God has also graciously brought several examples from Scripture to mind. It was after King David's baby died that he rose up from his mourning clothes, washed, anointed himself with oil and called for food. Those around him were baffled, as many are around us. David's response was that he would go to the baby in heaven, but the baby would never return to him (2 Samuel 12:19-23). God has chosen Trent to go home to heaven at this time; God has chosen us to live here at this time. May we always be faithful to God in the days that we have left to live and continue to do His work.

Another example is Jesus Christ himself, who Hebrews says suffered in many of the same ways that we have. He fully knew the consequences of sin and that God's plan for salvation would include death, even His own death on a cross. I have been recalling His reaction, and cannot ever recall when He was angry about it. Jesus struggled in the garden, but in the end it was God's will that He longed for over His own.

But my thoughts of Jesus also go to His resurrected body and give me, yet again, the hope of one day gladly giving up this body just as Trent has given up his body. I look forward all the more to the day that God calls me home. If I were in heaven I would not want to be wished back.

God reminded me of Lazarus and how Scripture says that Jesus wept. It is okay to weep.

Paul's life has also been on my mind over the last few days. At this time God has especially brought me the book of Philippians to affirm again His good plans in this. Paul was in prison facing his own death at the time, yet his only thought was to glorify God and to see many saved, which he did. Even in those circumstances, Paul says several times "Rejoice, and again, rejoice!" As the passage in Isaiah 65:17-25 was so sweetly given to us from God, I will hold on tightly to the verses that tell me this was God's good and perfect plan and it is okay to rejoice in it forever because that's what God is doing.

It feels as if we are being poured out like a drink offering, and like Paul, we can't choose which is better: to be with Christ or to remain here for the sake of God's work. Being that God has us here we can only choose to storm forth and battle for lost souls with a vengeance and an energy that we have never had before. We will continue to fight the good fight all the days that God allows us to do so. When and if the hard days come, I will worry about them then. Today God's grace is more than sufficient, and again today He has allowed me great rejoicing that my son is in heaven.

At this point I am trying to be very careful to let God handle all of the details as well. I tend to have my own ideas of how God should work even in this, and I need to remind myself over and over again that God will do the rest, not me. My part is to be faithful to what and to who He calls me, not to manage the numbers and times and depth that He will take people. It is God that I need to glorify, not my own ego.

I long to stay in this hiding place of God, where I am being carried by so many prayers and an abundance of grace, and where nothing else matters except the gospel going forth. The worldly things of jobs, money, schedules, etc., etc., are soon going to creep back in and I don't want to get caught up in this world again.

My other morning thoughts are of the amazing celebration that we enjoyed yesterday. I think of the numerous ministering opportunities that we had personally, and I am sure others had as well. Of the gospel going forth several times, personally and publicly. I think of the people who came to surround us. I tried to drink in every single part of the day, but at the same time let it all go and not hold on to the yesterdays so that we can do the work God would have for us in the tomorrows.

The finality is not Trent's body in the coffin. The finality is the work of God being done. No matter what God chooses to do with his death, Trent is still in heaven, and that will be enough. Although, I long for God to do more and to save many because that is what He promised to do. And He also promised to never leave me or forsake me in doing it. What a mighty God we serve!

I Realized When

February 26, 2011

I realized tonight just when this is going to get hard. It is going to get hard when I take my eyes off of the cross. That is when I will start to think that this is our final home. That is when I will forget where Trent is and what it cost for Jesus Himself to bring him there. I will start to forget that God Himself gave up His Son for my son to enter His glory. I will start to forget about God's perfect plan that He called "good". I will forget about the grace poured out on us on every step of this journey so far. I will forget that Trent was saved and is now in heaven. There were eleven other boys with Trent on that skiing trip, several who have admitted to us that they are not saved and would have been in hell right now had God taken them last Friday.

When my eyes stray from the cross my apathy returns and I forget the souls surrounding me that have an eternal destination. I will then seek my comfort here and expect again that this world will offer me what only God can provide. I will forget that my life is only as a shadow, that my eternity will be in heaven, and that only what is done for Christ will last.

I can say with Paul:

> Not that I have already obtained all this, or have already arrived at my goal, but I press on to take hold of that for which Christ Jesus took hold of me. Brothers and sisters, I do not consider myself yet to have taken hold of it. But one thing I do: Forgetting what is behind and straining toward what is ahead, I press on toward the goal to win the prize for which God has called me heavenward in Christ Jesus (Philippians 3:12-14).

May God never allow my eyes to stray from the cross in all of this. May He keep me faithful to the high calling that He has brought in my life. May it all be for His glory. And may many souls be woken up to answer the question: "What if it had been you that died on that slope on Friday? Where would you be?"

Where would your children be, Christian parent? Who are you raising them for? For the glory of God, or the glory of the world?

> Join together in following my example, brothers and sisters, and just as you have us as a model, keep your eyes on those who live as we do. For, as I have often told you before and now tell you again even with tears, many live as enemies of the cross of Christ. Their destiny is destruction, their god is their stomach, and their glory is in their shame. Their mind is set on earthly things. But our citizenship is in heaven. And we eagerly await a Savior from there, the Lord Jesus Christ, who, by the power that enables Him to bring everything under His control, will transform our lowly bodies so that they will be like his glorious body. Therefore, my brothers and sisters, you whom I love and long for, my joy and crown, stand firm in the Lord in this way, dear friends! Rejoice in the Lord always. I will say it again: Rejoice (Philippians 3:17-21, and 4:1,4)!

Struggling in the Garden

March 1, 2011

There has been just a bit of respite from the events of the past week and a half, and I have found that I am exhausted. My joy is still found in the Lord, and knowing that Trent is in heaven only causes smiles, but my human body is worn out. Graciously, God allowed a couple of nights with solid sleep, plus a long nap yesterday.

Everything seems to take extra effort just to accomplish at this point. The gifts of meals, paper plates, pizza, coffee, and friends who came to sweep my floors and fold my laundry have been all the more appreciated. At this point we are gearing up to handle more details. Bills are waiting to get paid, arrangements for releasing Trent's ashes over his birthday next week have to be planned, and eventually the Xbox vacation needs to end for the younger kids.

I have deliberately been looking up passages in Scripture that refer to God's will and heaven, affirming again that God's plan is perfect and what He is bringing forth from Trent's death is perfect. The book of Job has been especially comforting. Satan may have intended this for evil, but God is using it for His good and has already brought salvation. My struggle is not with God or His plan for Friday. My struggle at this point is how do I go on living the same after Friday?

God had been convicting us that we were too caught up in this world before He took Trent home, but now we are all the more convinced that nothing matters except for what is done for Christ. As Rob said at the celebration, "All of Trent's guns and everything he loved is still here, the only thing in heaven is his soul." I look around at all the things that mattered so much, and have a hard time making them look so valuable now. On the contrary, I look around and see all the foolishness and false living that people are so caught up in, and find myself begging God even more to open their eyes, along with mine.

I find myself torn between asking God to leave us here to minister to all those around us who He has given for us to be salt and light, and asking Him to allow us to give up all these earthly possessions and take us into full-time ministry with no earthly ties. I am tired of spending all my energy and putting all my emotions into paying the mortgage when there are souls that are perishing all around me. I long to build with precious stone and jewels that my life may stand the test of God's refining fire.

> Do not store up for yourselves treasures on earth, where moth and rust destroy, and where thieves break in and steal. But store up for yourselves treasures in heaven, where moth and rust do not destroy, and where thieves do not break in and steal. For where your treasure is, there your heart will be also (Matthew 6:19-21).

I Miss Him

March 2, 2011

I have found myself missing Trent so much the last couple of days. I miss his smile. I miss how he came up and rubbed my lower back with his fist. I miss how he was always there as my protector, whether I was talking with somebody or just trying to do something, he sensed it and was right there. I miss how he crawled into my bed and snuggled in the morning. I miss how he always said, "Goodnight Mom, love you." I miss seeing him lying in his bed, waiting for his blessing, asking to snuggle. I miss how he always wanted to stay up late to watch Star Wars, and especially wanted me to stay up late with him. I miss how he loved to cook and was always whipping up something extra special, even if I didn't always like the extra seasonings or the wild game of the day. I miss his help in the barn, how he jumped in to do the heavy work. I miss him being here when the goats are born. I miss not seeing him roam the woods. I miss not seeing him ride his bike, or the 4-wheeler, or the snowmobile, or the short horses. I miss his giggle. I miss him not being here to clean the kitchen or do the dishes on Monday. I miss how he hated schoolwork and would only work hard on it so he could earn computer time or go outside. I miss his Bible questions. I miss his spiky hair-do and his long Ken-doll locks. I miss how he would be forced to shower only to have to go back and wash his hair in the sink because he "forgot" to wash it in the shower. I miss his long fingernails that he hated to trim. I miss all the holey shirts that he chose to wear over anything nice. I miss him coming down the steps in the morning in his PJ's. I miss him fighting with his brothers and sisters. I miss him talking with Lexi at night after he was supposed to be tucked in bed. I miss his horrible printing and spelling. I miss him teasing me about wearing his socks. I miss him running down to the barn in his underwear with Cole in the winter because they wanted to beat the guys in the movie, "8 Below". I miss him taking pictures. I miss him having fun with Thomas and Samuel. I miss him working for Russell and asking for a raise. I miss him looking at his hunting magazines and browsing the bait and tackle rows at Walmart. I miss him playing football and working so hard for his coaches. I just plain old miss him, and eternity seems so far away. But I know where he is, and I still wouldn't want him back for a day. Lord, haste the day that I see my son again. Be my comforter as You promised to be. I do trust You in this and love that Your ways are perfect.

Just Some Encouragement

March 2, 2011

For the past year or so the book by my bedside has been *Filling up the Afflictions of Christ: The Cost of Bringing the Gospel to the Nations in the Lives of William Tyndale, Adoniram Judson, and John Paton* by John Piper. For some reason I have struggled to get into the meat of the book—maybe because I really didn't want to know the cost of bringing the gospel to the nations? Yet every time I saw it lying there I felt it's calling to learn the cost.

This morning as I was longing for encouragement in what God is doing, I picked up the book, my Bible, a big cup of coffee, and crawled into the recliner. I re-read the story of John Paton, reading a bit more carefully the part about when he had first gone to the island of Tanna and within the first four months of being there both his wife and his newborn son died of a sudden illness.

In the sorrow of losing the two most precious people in his life he was consoled by the fact that he never had to doubt that his wise and loving Father would ever make a mistake in anything that He does or permits. Fifteen years later, after losing another child, he could still hold on to the fact that Jesus never made mistakes. He looked forward to one day being in heaven when he would understand fully how God was glorified in everything He chose to do.

What powerful words to remember today as I look up to the Lord for help and continue to struggle on in His work.

The Alien Planet

March 4, 2011

As Traci would say, "Day 14 on the Alien Planet." That's about how it feels—like we are walking around in a different zone than anybody else.

We had to make a Walmart trip tonight because my contacts were (ahem) 6 months overdue and I couldn't put off getting a new pair any longer. I was doing pretty well until we were waiting in line to check in and I saw the doctors name. What are the odds that his name would be Trent, too? Then the oblivious, young doctor made some comment about bringing all the kids along and the next thing you know he has a crying lady on his hands.

At home it's one thing to be able to wander around trying to figure out just how to keep putting one foot in front of the other, but going out in the real world again baffles me. I watch people and think, "Don't you know that my son just died? Don't you know that it could be your son, or you, next? Does eternity not matter more than what's on sale at Walmart?" And then I have to make a choice between root beer or orange pop, bottles or cans, to take on a trip to spread my son's ashes next week. Bizarre.

And that's about all I have to say about that. I'm going to go finish off the cheese puffs and see if I can make it through one more Star Wars movie in the Great Star Wars Movie Fest in honor of Trent.

Being Where We Are

March 12, 2011

What a journey God has us on. The thoughts, prayers, and theology that have gone through my mind, besides all of the events of the past three weeks, has my mind trying to organize God's intricate workings together into a pretty little package so that I can sit down one day and just sort everything out. The God who I didn't realize I had in a nice little box of my own has revealed Himself to be more than I could have ever imagined Him to be.

His promises have been more real than they have ever been before and His peace has been beyond anything I could ever imagine. The words that He has whispered in my ears, or shouted from billboards, or spoken through friends and strangers have been a balm to soothe my pain to the point that I wonder if I should be sadder that Trent is in heaven rather than here.

I am not in denial, I know Trent is gone and I miss him like crazy, but the overwhelming knowledge of God being in control is my constant compass to point me heavenward in everything that tries to take away this joy. Yes, joy. Joy that goes beyond anything this world has to offer and joy deeper than any sorrow. My delight is in the Lord and His plans. He has allowed complete surrender to my own ways in this and has replaced it with peace. Where else do I have to turn but the Lord, the Maker of heaven and earth?

Just because He is kind to His children He has led me to several verses that have brought, again, the reassurance that God is good and is definitely in control of all of this. And without a doubt He loves me throughout it and in it.

From Isaiah 48 and 57:1-2

My own hand laid the foundations of the earth, and my right hand spread out the heavens; when I summon them, they all stand together. (If we serve a God who could simply form the earth and the heavens by speaking, then we have to believe that this God also ordained the day of the accident perfectly as well, and all for His glory.)

This is what the Lord says~ your Redeemer, the Holy One of Israel; I am the Lord your God, who teaches you what is best for you, who directs you in the way you should go. If only you had paid attention to my commands, your peace would have been like a river, your righteousness like the waves of the sea. (You have allowed me to pay attention to your commands, Oh Lord, and my peace is like a river!)

For my own sake, for my own sake, I do this {declares the Lord}. How can I let myself be defamed? I will not yield my glory to another. Listen to me, you islands; hear this, you distant nations: Before I was born the Lord called me; from my birth he has made mention of my name. He made my mouth like a sharpened sword, in the shadow of his hand he hid me; he made me into a polished arrow and concealed me in his quiver.

The righteous perish, and no one ponders it in his heart; devout men are taken away, and no one understands that the righteous are taken away to be spared from evil. Those who walk uprightly enter into peace; they find rest as they lie in death.

Isaiah 59:1 *Surely the arm of the Lord is not too short to save, nor his ear too dull to hear.*

Time in Scripture

March 15, 2011

I love my husband. I love God for His wisdom in making Rob my husband. I love how he holds such high regard for the Word of God and obedience to it. I love how together we are remembering the promises of God to His children and being encouraged by what He has in store for us. Pondering the God whose ways are not our ways. Rejoicing in His plans for our lives. Trusting Him to be faithful until we see Him face to face.

> *How sweet are your words to my taste, sweeter than honey to my mouth! Psalm 119:103*

Still Here

March 21, 2011

I wake up every day and Trent is still in heaven. The various range of emotions go from elation to uncontrollable tears. I hate crying. I don't know why, I just have never been a crier and I don't know how to do it well. Maybe it's the loss of composure, or my need for control. Maybe it's because of the facade of my own strength that I don't want revealed. The tears come easier now which "they" tell me is good. I should be crying, "they" say. I make people uncomfortable if I don't cry. But I make myself uncomfortable if I do cry.

Quit being such a people pleaser, Terri, and be where God has you today, right now. Trent is in heaven; I would not wish him back. But I see him everywhere. I miss him. I long for him. I ache to feel him in my arms. Somehow I have to learn how to live again. The things of this world have failed to bring any charm or joy.

Only the things of God hold any hope. To hear the stories of changed lives already brings great joy. The numerous people with whom we have been privileged to share the gospel give this a purpose. To think of Trent, free from the bondage of his sin, standing in awe of his Savior, looking face to face with his Creator makes me smile. This is not about me. But somehow "me" has to live here doing the good works that God has ordained until my day comes to go home.

This Journey

March 26, 2011

This journey has led me to places that I could not fathom going.

It has also lead me to knowing and trusting God in a way that I could not imagine. Pondering just who God is and why He does what He does. Looking at Scripture with a whole different meaning. Loving the promises with a whole different depth. Counting on God to really do what He says He will do in His time.

God has taken me to a different height and asked if I still trust Him.

Do I really believe that He is leading me by the hand as we walk it together?

Am I going to let go?

Can I trust Him and let Him be God with His plans for my life and not my own?

By His grace I will keep looking up and keep saying, "Yes Lord, Your will be done, not mine. Take me where You please because Your ways are not my ways and Your plans are not my plans. Yours are better, and I surrender all to You."

Just Sayin'

March 26, 2011

Pastor Doug started his sermon at the funeral by saying {in my recollection}: "Funerals are hard. You never know what to say to those left behind. My advice, though, is that if your cat or your dog just died don't tell Rob and Terri that you know what they are going through. You don't know." Of course, we all laughed. Of course, Doug has been to a few more funerals than I have and knew what was to come in the many days ahead.

We are beyond the stage where everybody who sees us hugs us. We are not quite to the stage where most people forgot that we ever had a 12-year-old son. We are in the stage where nobody knows quite what to say to us (except, of course, those few brave souls who give up their mornings or their children's lunch hour or their ice cream time to ask) so it's easier to not say anything at all lest they have blubbering parents on their hands or we start sputtering about Jesus and salvation and heaven and all that again.

So if you chat with me and I don't quite get excited over new faucets or the agony of what color to choose for the third bathroom or the hangnail on your big left toe that has been dangling for a week . . . Know that I still care, it's just that I am probably trying to process things like which clothes of Trent's are sentimental to keep and which ones should I donate to Goodwill? What were my last words to my son and what will be my first ones? Will that insurance company really cover all the expenses or do we have to dip into our savings or the memorial money that we long to use to honor God so that the gospel can go forth even more?

Somehow priorities have changed a bit for us. Faucets still leak and hangnails still hang, but when your son just entered heaven they don't seem to hold the same weight anymore. Give us time, ask us how we are, we'll try not to get your shoulder too wet and pretty soon we'll care about glossy or satin finish again.

Or maybe God will keep eternity very close to our minds and hearts and we will ask you yet again, "Where would you be if it had been you that Friday? Are you ready to meet your Creator? Do you know His Son Jesus?"

Today

March 27, 2011

Today I am trying to imagine heaven. I can look out my window and see snow on the fields, physical buildings half done and waiting for finishing touches, animals contentedly eating their hay, young boys' bikes waiting to be ridden. But I cannot envision heaven. I cannot begin to fathom where Trent is or what he is seeing.

Though I lived so intimately with him for his whole 12 years, I cannot imagine where he is right now. It's a bit different than dropping him off at summer camp for a week, seeing which cabin he's in, meeting his counselor, and watching him head off to the lake to go fishing. That whole week I can envision the wakeup bell ringing and sleepy boys pulling their clothes on to hurry to the dining hall for breakfast, singing in chapel, playing with friends, enjoying the games, and sitting around campfires at dusk.

How can I begin to imagine what Trent is experiencing, and has experienced, the past several weeks. "Where are you, Trent?" was the first question that ran through my mind when I saw his body at the hospital. I knew where he was when he wandered the woods at home in search of pheasants or squirrels. I knew where he was when he went to shovel snow at Russell's house and sat down in his kitchen for coffee and cookies. I knew where he was every morning as I sat in the recliner reading my Bible and he lay in his bed, sleeping safely. I had been where he was.

But where are you now, my son? What is heaven like? Are you talking with Gideon about the battles of long ago? Are you discussing ancient weaponry, and the might and glory of God to send so many home that the victory would be won with God's strength alone? Are you talking to Enoch or Elijah asking if they are the prophets who will return? Are you asking Paul about the stonings, about the scales, about the shipwreck? Or are you still just standing in awe of the God and Savior that your mother could never have come close to describing to you?

One day you were here, Trent, the next you were at the throne of God. How I long to know what heaven is like so that I may envision where you are. How I long to stand in awe with you, praising the God who gives and takes away.

Lord, I need your reality today. Show me, again, Yourself. Comfort me with Your peace. Send me Your Words which I count on to endure.

Today I will listen all the more for the trumpet call and watch closer for my Savior to return. When the good works that He has prepared for me to do here are done, and when my duties that bring glory to His name are done, I too will know what heaven is like. The earth and everything in it will fade away, but the name of the Lord will endure forever. Lord haste the day when You make all things right for Your glory.

Rocket Science

March 29, 2011

At this point making pancakes is like rocket science. I think we're somewhere in that hazy brain stage of grief. One egg, two eggs. Whole batch or double batch? Oh yes, Trent is in heaven, one and a half batches will be plenty. Whisk. Add milk, sugar, flour, and baking powder. Mix some more. Pour. Add blueberries. Flip. Butter. Repeat. Another meal completed. What was my name again?

But How Are You Really Doing?

March 30, 2011

Although I constantly answer by saying, "God is good and that's what counts," it is inevitably followed up with "But how are you really doing? It's okay to cry, you should be grieving, don't you miss him, you don't have to pretend to be strong for us, you can't really be doing well when your son just died, it seems fake." Well people, I don't know how else to be except how God has me right now. I laughed after I pondered the fake comment. Not sure how I could fake being happy to hundreds of people and myself and my immediate family for so long without cracking somewhere.

Of course I am crying; he's my son. Of course I miss him; he's my son. Of course I am grieving; he's my son. I am a people-pleaser at the core so could easily find myself pretending for others' sakes, but more than being a people-pleaser God is turning me into a God-pleaser first. If I am pretending I am pretending to myself pretty well, too, because every morning I have woken up since the accident, the first words on my lips are: "Thank you, God, that Trent is in heaven." And at the end of the day it is still my son who is not here. What good would it do to pretend away that fact?

But honestly . . . God is good and that's what counts. We are trusting in His plan for this. Odd, I know; call us kooks, but we really do believe every word in the Bible. Especially the passages that talk about God's sovereignty, salvation, heaven, that this world will pass as a shadow, eternity is a long, long time and God really does have a grand plan to glorify His name in all of this.

My dear Christian sister and brother, do we believe the Bible or not? Is there anything that escapes God? Could He not have prevented this if He wanted to? Does He really ordain the day of our death? Is heaven better than this world? Can we really trust what God does with our lives? Doesn't He promise peace and strength to His children as they obey Him and cling to Him, even in hard times, especially in hard times?

Why then are we such an oddity? What if all that God promises only comes true? Doesn't He promise to never leave us or forsake us? Doesn't He promise peace like a river when we obey His commands? Then let our oddity in rejoicing over God's plan be a wake up call to believers and non-believers alike.

To the non-believers: that you might take the time to stop and consider the day of your own death when you, too, will meet your Creator. There are no second chances after death, and there are no guarantees to the number of days that we think we are entitled to here on this earth. It is only by Jesus that we are saved and able to enter heaven, and I understand that Hell is not a fun place to be. Last I heard, we are all guaranteed to die unless that trumpet call comes first.

To the believers: Wake up. Please wake up.

Why do we think that God is required to give us cotton candy and pony rides during our passing days on this earth? Do you not understand that you are on enemy territory? This is a fallen world ruled by Satan himself. Do you not understand that you cannot sit idle in the midst of a war? Do you not realize that there are high costs and the casualties will hit close to your heart? Where in Scripture are we guaranteed a spot on the Lazy Boy recliner while the battle is being fought? Are you fighting?

Do you realize that the enemy is right outside your door, even in your own home, in your living room? Sin is crouching and longs to master you, dear one. Where will you turn in the day of your own testing if you have not built your foundation now? What god are you serving? Are you serving the God of the Bible? Do you know Him? Do you know His Word and His promises and His warnings? He's not kidding. One day it will be you who stands before His throne.

He has offered freedom my friends. Freedom from our sins, freedom to serve Him, freedom to suffer for Him because it brings Him glory in a way that we cannot understand this side of heaven. Choose this day whom you will serve because it does have eternal consequences. This freedom is only found in the blood of Jesus Christ on the cross. There is no other way. If He is beckoning today, answer today, because there may not be another tomorrow or another beckoning. Wake up: please, wake up.

Do you know what God requires to enter heaven? Perfection according to His standards. He considers hatred to be murder. He considers lust to be adultery. He does not share His glory with whatever idol we create. We have become masters in denying our own sinfulness, but God sees through it and hasn't forgotten. For all have sinned (yes, even you and me babe) and fallen short of the glory of God. There is nothing we can do in and of ourselves to make ourselves right with God. The only hope is to beg Him to save our wretched selves. And He says that He will.

God says that all who call on the name of Jesus Christ, those who believe in His name and what He did on the cross, will be saved. Our sins were laid upon the very Son of God on that cross. Jesus was the perfect sacrifice that God required for payment and forgiveness so that we may enter into His presence. But it's not about raising your hand at the campfire to accept Jesus into your heart. He also says that you need to deny yourself, pick up your cross, and follow Him, no matter the cost (Luke 9:23).

What does this mean without the "Christianese"? It means that you give it all up. Your pride in saving yourself, your plans for your own idea of the perfect American lifestyle, your own ideas of God. You must surrender all. It means letting God lead in His way, letting Him be Lord over your life, letting Him forgive you.

But, oh, how deep our sin and our pride go. How we would rather stubbornly hold on to our own ways and our own plans and shake our fist at God than let His plan for salvation be so easy. Rather than seeking the Bible to learn who this God is, we have replaced Him with a health-and-wealth gospel and the latest book or idea. Rather than a sovereign God who is coming again to judge the world for all her sins, we have created a Santa-Claus-in-the-sky grandfather who winks at our sins. God says He loves His children, but He will not tolerate their sin.

Is He sanctifying you? Are you becoming more like Christ as laid out in Scripture? Search your hearts and know where you are with God. Only those who endure to the end will be saved. May we be willing to fight the good fight at all costs and bring honor to our God by holding onto His Word. Wake us up, Lord, that we might reveal You to this dark world.

Some Days

April 3, 2011

Some days I forget what the fight is about. Some days I forget that God is sovereign. Some days I wish that Trent were still here. Some days I torture myself with the thoughts of the things that he won't be here for. Some days I look at trails through the snow and realize that he will never walk those trails. Some days I look at the places he was, and now is not. Some days I hate it that the toothpaste tube that was full when he was alive now needs to be thrown away. Some days I hate it that I have to use Colgate now instead of Aquafresh because somebody was so kind as to bring us toothpaste because our son died. Some days I hate sin more than other days because sin lead to death. Some days I forget how to put one foot in front of the other.

But then, those days, God sends His Word again. God sends His children to minister again. God turns my eyes to the cross again. God brings me back to where it all matters. Not here, but eternity. Not me, but Him. Not now, but then.

Then, when He will ransom those that are His. Then, when there will be no more tears. Then, when those dead in Christ will rise first and there will be no more death. Then, when all that the locust destroyed will be restored. Then, when all those that were brought to Christ through the death of one 12-year-old boy will be revealed. Then, when those rich rewards will be given out, only to be laid at the feet of my Savior because He will be enough.

Some days, everyday, God really is more than sufficient to turn my eyes back to Him when they look to the here and now to be the balm. Today, again, I will cling to my Rock.

Faith Like a Child

April 3, 2011

To watch a child is to understand God on a whole different level. Jesus said that unless we change and become like little children, we would not enter heaven (Matthew 18:3). Is salvation really as hard as we want to make it out to be? Is trusting God really that difficult? Did He say it? Then why don't we believe it and simply live like He instructed?

Traci shared with me that the day after the accident, when the house was overflowing and the multitude of kids were all enjoying the party, one of her six children came to her and said they couldn't find Trent. She explained to them again that Trent had died and was in heaven, remember? Oh that's right, and off they went to play. Total trust. God said it, God did it, keep living, keep laughing, keep believing, keep smiling.

Let me sit at your feet and learn of your God, little one's.

But Who's Going to Eat all the Ramen Noodles?

April 5, 2011

The party is winding down. Most of the people have gone home. The amount of tomato and hamburger hot dishes is dwindling in the freezer. There is an end in sight to the stack of thank you cards that I am still working on. Reality is setting in, and Trent is still in heaven. My brain is still foggy and slow most days, and little things bring me back again to the reality that he is gone.

Walking sticks that he was working on, a card that he forgot to give me, letters in the classroom mailbox, a picture on the fridge, a glimpse of the remembrance of his smile and kisses. Looking in the pantry and realizing that one day I will have to go grocery shopping again and make the big decisions of what kind of cereal to buy and how many bags of tater tots we need.

The little things that made the big differences are being realized. The boy who loved Ramen noodles when the rest of us only tolerated them is gone. That blue box will sit for months on the pantry shelf as a reminder. The school books he left behind, as well as the dirty laundry that will sneak it's way into the washer, will bring back the reality over and over again.

The house is a little quieter, and cleaner if you ask Traci, even though the dishes still don't get done on Monday's or the kitchen floor swept. My heart still aches and tears wet my face. Thank the Lord that He protects us from this being an overwhelming flood that longs to destroy. Though the waters come up to our neck they will go no further. Our God has ordained His plans perfectly, and again we will rejoice in them.

Plain Old Hard Work

April 7, 2011

Grief is just plain old hard work. Physical work, I am a master at. I tend to be too good at physical work most of the time, and enjoy taking on more than I think I can handle. Grief is hard, emotional work. It overwhelms every part of life and consumes you until you deal with it. There are no coffee breaks and there is no way around it. From day one I have determined to go barreling straight through, facing everything head-on rather than sidestepping and dealing with it twenty years later. Eyes wide open, heart revealed, God leading me. On the hard days I resort back to the physical work. My house is now free from a minimum of a dozen full garbage bags, plus box after box of junk and recycled items. Anything that wasn't nailed down or was worn out or we haven't used in months is gone. My floors have been swept and re-swept and I made the kids join me in cleaning out the classroom that had become a junk collection spot for months. It felt good to turn the emotional work into something that produced results. We all laughed at me and how I am, and agreed that Trent must be extra glad to be in heaven now rather than cleaning the dreaded classroom closet.

A Balancing Act

April 9, 2011

Grief is a balancing act. All those articles and books don't even come close to describing it. Reading through the pages or paragraphs that talk about the 5 steps, or the 7 steps, or the 12 steps don't leave much room for the days that you can't figure out which step you are on or if there is even a step for where you are. Which step is it that you just want your son back but you know above all else that God has something better planned and that one day He will make it right but today you can't seem to remember that for all you're worth?

Some days just staying on top is too much. Some days I just want to hold Trent again, and see his smile, and hear his voice this side of eternity. I want to know where he is, what he's doing, all the things he is experiencing. I want to trust God to wait. I want His reminders again. I want to quit crying. I want to remember that God's ways are not my ways and that they really are better. I want to remember that God had this all ordained and one day I won't remember how much it cost and how much it hurts.

As I am right where God wants me, I want to rejoice in the work that He is doing through this. Through the tears and the pain and the hurt. Let the tears flow because my heavenly Father is bottling them up, crying with me. Let my heart break, for He holds it in His hands. Did He not give up His own Son? Has He asked me any more? Not more, but less. I want to remember that I am in the palm of His hand. There are no "ifs" or "accidents" in God's plans.

I want the rejoicing again, God. I want the flood of trust again, God. I want the peace again, God. I want my eyes on the cross again, God. Let me quit trying to figure this out, God, and just be where You have me today. Today You are faithful. Today You are sufficient. Today You love me and have plans for my good. Today is enough. You are enough, God.

So Soon

April 11, 2011

I had to work the first Sunday of 2011. Rob shared with me that Pastor Doug had given his regular New Year's sermon which included the unsettling warning that some of us this year would be affected by death, possibly even our own death, and to consider seriously where we were with Jesus Christ and what we were living our lives for. The thought never crossed our minds that it would be our son that would not make it to 2012.

Just a couple of days after Trent died, Rob ran into a coworker at the grocery store who of course offered her condolences and was so sorry for us. Rob shared our joy that Trent was in heaven because of the salvation offered through Jesus on the cross and asked where she would be had she died. Then she was in a hurry and had to get going.

She came to the funeral and heard the gospel message preached several times, the sweet words of the offer of eternity in heaven if she would just repent and surrender her life to the Lord. This woman had just come out of a long battle with cancer that it appeared she had overcome, so the thought of death had been on her mind for several months already. She was one of the many that we had been praying for salvation as she sat in the pews listening to the message that day. Rob finished the celebration by laying out the gospel clearly one more time and told the 400-plus people that it was a real possibility that the next time he saw one of them they would be in a coffin.

Last Friday, just weeks after Trent's accident and hearing the gospel so many times, this lady finished off her work day and told her co-workers, "See you on Monday." But she is not coming back to work today because she died suddenly over the weekend. No warning, just gone.

Gone to face her Maker who graciously warned her repeatedly to call on His name. Gone without any evidence that she ever took the time to stop running and call on Jesus' name. The time is so short and hearts get so hard so fast. How we are burdened for those who have heard our message but choose to deny Christ or to put it off until tomorrow to decide. Today, if you hear His voice beckoning with salvation, do not delay. There are no guarantees of tomorrow. Eternity is a long time. Praying that God may choose to bless you with salvation today.

Because It's What I Know How To Do

April 11, 2011

Taking pictures is what I know how to do. It's not as difficult as thinking hard and having to decide what to cook for supper these days. Or which clothes to put in the washing machine. Or what I should do with Trent's trophies. Taking pictures again, though, has proven to be difficult.

It's difficult because of the guilt. Guilt that I was enjoying something without Trent being here. How could life go on, the grass get green, the family still be a family and have fun and create new memories to take pictures of without Trent here?

How could I be just two months after the death of my son and live life without him?

Because of four other children who need a mother and need memories. Because God is gracious. Because it is healing. Because God has my day to die planned as well as He had Trent's and it wasn't February 18, 2011. Because Trent lived while he was here and taught me how to do it. Because whether I take pictures or not he is still in heaven. Because there are still a lot of things to take pictures of. Because I want to remember. Because I want them to remember me.

ℬlack and White

April 12, 2011

Blah! My brain is on strike. I can't think up a creative building project or even get the gumption to go clean out another closet. I am in black and white mode. I try to spend time in Scripture pondering the sweet truths and promises, but mostly my eyes focus on some far away place and I am in a daze. There is a deep strength and hope in my Savior that He knows exactly what He's doing, and that carries me through the day. But the day that I mostly think about is the Day that God will make all things right again.

I know that I do not walk this journey alone. God is leading me by the hand. But I also know that there are four children and a husband walking it as well. The pain of watching your husband cry over his son is often times harder than crying yourself. The comfort of sharing new found verses and revelations and dreams with your daughter makes the way a little easier. Young children who still believe in happily ever after and want you to believe, too, bring me out of the daze for a bit.

And then come the bills and the insurance claims and the old t-shirts in the hamper to make me realize that even through the fog life must go on. I find myself thanking God for this foggy stage of grief that the brain might have a chance to catch up to what the soul already knows. I find myself praising God when the fog does clear for a bit and just holding on by my fingertips until it lifts again.

God knows the paths that He has laid out for me and I will gladly walk them because He has asked me to, missing my son and all, because I know it is with my Savior that I walk until I see him again.

Really Paul??

April 17, 2011

I consider that our present sufferings are not worth comparing with the glory that will be revealed in us.

And we know that in all things God works for the good of those who love Him, who have been called according to His purpose.

For those God foreknew, He also predestined to be conformed to the likeness of His Son, that He might be the firstborn among many brothers.

And those He predestined, He also called;
those He called, He also justified;
those He justified, He also glorified.

In all these things we are more than conquerors through Him who loves us.

Taken from Romans 8.

Perspectives

April 17, 2011

Perspectives. To look at things from a different angle. How can you imagine something you could never imagine?

Watching the old maple tree form it's spring buds somehow sums up the past two months in my life. It marks time in a way that I could never have realized it would. To think back through the decades when this tree must have started and survived in the middle of my cow pasture to grow to the monstrous maple it is today to be a reminder to me right now is beyond my comprehension. It is just a tree. But he was my son.

The last project that Trent and I worked on together was tapping that maple tree. Just days before he died we dreamed about the sap of life that would flow from this tree. About the days of checking for full buckets. About sitting around a campfire and waiting for the liquid to change consistency and turn into sweet syrup. To have tried and achieved, or even tried and failed, at another project together. About enjoying the fruit of our labor.

But somehow this tree has gone on to see another spring and Trent is gone. I didn't have the heart to collect the sap that flowed. I let it run on the ground before I could make myself go out and pull the taps that Trent had put in. When I saw the new buds forming on the tree I wanted to ask it, "How can you live? How can you bloom? Don't you know? Don't you know that he's gone?"

What seemed like just another project has become a treasured memory. What was just another day turned into eternity. What was just Mom taking more pictures turned into treasured pieces of art.

I find I hold every event closer now. I find I hold my children closer, as well as my husband, and my friends, and my family. I take more pictures than ever before and treasure every moment more than before. Not because they will bring Trent back, but because I don't want to miss a single detail on this journey that God has me on to create His own masterpiece. I don't want to miss the little details that He is weaving in my life for His glory. I want to look back and see His fingerprints all over everything. Not missing one little thing or taking it for granted. I want to see it from God's perspective. The hurt, the pain, the joy, the growth, the blooms and all.

Dancing Again

April 23, 2011

I'm not quite sure just where to start this post or where it will wind up, so bear with me for some rambling. It's more of a collection of thoughts, prayers, reminders and the direction of what God has been doing the past few days in my life. Oh, lonesome me, I have been a bit whiny and pathetic lately, believe it or not. I've lost sight, in a sense, of God's hand. I have started to enjoy wallowing in my own self-pity rather than trust the Creator of the universe to do good things in my life.

Nobody ever told me that grief was so exhausting. I find I hardly do anything and am exhausted by the mere thought of just thinking. Thinking about . . . I don't even know what. It can hardly even be called thinking because the thoughts don't connect anywhere. Simply recalling and treasuring memories. Dazing and processing. The kids or Rob will ask me a question and it sounds like Greek. Questions just baffle me for a moment. Huh?

147

I have realized that the brain goes into shock after losing somebody you love. Slowly, slowly that shock seems to wear off and bits and pieces come flooding back of what just happened. Hard nights of odd thoughts and dreams and fear that make you hold your husband to make sure that he is still there and not a cold body. For unknown reasons, at any odd time of the day, the fresh realization that Trent died. As if I didn't already know that.

We were spared seeing any trauma of Trent's death, but the trauma still takes its toll. Tears come without expecting them over silly things. I see Trent's face in strangers and hear his voice in my mind. Then there are the days that I can hardly conjure up his smile or imagine his giggle or the twinkle in his eye when he got excited about something, like talking about God.

The ache of missing Trent that there is no cure for is nearly constant. The odd, dull, no emotion, flat-line approach to everything. Nothing thrills like it used to. Not the sunsets, or the frogs croaking, or the bags of groceries. The new green grass barely registers a shimmer of joy and what does it matter if it's rainy or sunny?

Aah! How did I get so sidetracked? How did I forget Who's in charge? When did I stop reciting the Promises? When did my eyes stray from the cross? How easy it is to forget, to lose hope, to look to the immediate to be the eternal.

When I am tired it's easier to get discouraged. When I have no mission or purpose it's easier. Everybody wants to spare me from anything extra at this time, but the extras are what I need to keep sane. Having something to do, like minister to twenty kids and nearly that many adults in my home, allows my mind a break. And then my sweet mom, who does her best to spare me any pain, tells me of the dear ladies at work who are worried about me and send their hugs and gifts. Tears again. Good tears. Cleansing, happy, sad, joyful tears. Tears for myself, not for

Trent. Tears because he is my son. Tears because I miss him and long to be where he is.

And how do you reconcile living without it being dishonoring to the person who died? Guilt is Satan's playground in a woman's life. Is trusting God not enough of a reason to keep on living? Simply believing that in His wisdom there is a reason for me to be left at this time. What good am I curled up on the couch in the fetal position? Can I not go on living and walking in faith? Looking for the good works that must be left for me to do here? Accepting what God has done and calling it good; trusting His plans above my own; not my will, but God's be done?

Cole and I went on our big grocery shopping trip the other day. The last time I went was the week or so before Trent died. On that trip I almost brought the camera, but as it is such a normal thing in our life, I thought, "How silly! We do this all the time!" How I wish I had. How I wish I had taken a thousand more pictures, recorded and saved every silly video, wrote down every normal thing Trent had said during his short years here.

I thought I was ready for the real world. But I saw Trent everywhere. To pass the rows of shirts his size, seeing something he would like, and being reminded yet again. Picturing him in the seat next to me holding the Papa Murphy's pizza. Watching him pick the pickles off his double cheeseburger and then offering me the last french fry.

Blah, grief, go away. Oh death, where is your victory, oh death, where is your sting? My God ordained even this perfectly. All this heartache and every tear will be made right by the One who made them. When His work is done in this sinful world all will be revealed and made right. The riches of His glory will be made known to the objects of His mercy through this. Patience. Patience. I long to walk in this fallen world holding tightly to my Savior until that day.

God came to my rescue again. He pulled me out of the miry, dirty, sticky, gooey clay that I had done a pretty fine job of sinking myself into. His Word penetrated deep into my heart again. Prayers with a faithful husband who loves me and puts up with more than he deserves started to remind me again of what the fight is about. It is about God's glory. What did He say? Why do I listen to my deceiving heart? Put it into perspective, oh heart. Trust God's Word.

And friends, dear friends, God used your prayers and the words that you were so faithful to share in mighty ways: the reminders, the perspectives, the encouragement. You truly are sharing my burden and we carry it together, making it lighter. His yoke is easy when we obey. Shoshannah left the words that shook me out of what I was doing. It put things into perspective again. She reminded me to dance before my King. Where had all my joy gone? I literally found a kid or two and danced! To their joy, laughter, and shaking heads!

My son is in heaven! Shout it from the rooftop! PRAISE the Lord! My son is in heaven! Stop doubting and believe, oh me of little faith! God knows what He is doing, and He has called it good.

Romans 8:9

You, however, are controlled not by the sinful nature but by the Spirit, if the Spirit lives in you.

Romans 8:18-25

I consider that our present sufferings are not worth comparing with the glory that will be revealed in us. The creation waits in eager expectation for the sons of God to be revealed. For the creation was subjected to frustration, not by its own choice, but by the will of the one who subjected it, in hope that the creation itself will be liberated from its bondage to decay and brought into the glorious freedom of the children of God.

We know that the whole creation has been groaning as in the pains of childbirth right up to the present time. Not only so, but we ourselves, who have the first fruits of the Spirit, groan inwardly as we wait eagerly for our adoption as sons, the redemption of our bodies. For in this hope we were saved. But hope that is seen is no hope at all. Who hopes for what he already has? But if we hope for what we do not yet have, we wait for it patiently.

Acts 3:21

He must remain in heaven until the time comes for God to restore everything, as He promised long ago through His holy prophets.

Revelation 22:12 and 20b

Behold, I am coming soon! My reward is with me, and I will give to everyone according to what he has done. ~ Yes, I am coming soon. {Jesus}

How is it Possible?

April 27, 2011

How is it possible to miss somebody this much?

Normal

April 28, 2011

"Normal" scares me lately more than anything else. Take today for instance: Rob went to work, the kids and I enjoyed coffee, breakfast, and our quiet Bible time. We completed nearly a full day of home school, Cole helped me do outside chores while the other kids cleaned up the house, we enjoyed lunch, went to piano lessons, and I talked to a friend on the phone. I worked outside on farm stuff with Rob after work while the kids played, had supper, then family devotions and got the kids tucked into bed. Just normal stuff.

Normal stuff without Trent. The new normal. And somehow it was okay. My thoughts were never very far away from the knowledge of Trent being in heaven, but God gave me such a peace today to somehow live and function doing normal life things. What else do you do? Cry all day like yesterday? Some "normal" might not be so bad.

Free Falling

April 30, 2011

I sit here this morning reading your comments, friends, and see first hand all over again how good God is to our family. Comments like Sonja's about how God has laid Cole on her heart lately and how she has faithfully prayed for him brought tears to my eyes. Friends like Cathy, who responded with a covering of prayer and a sweet email to check on me after God's prompting on the day that just "happened" to be when I opened the mailbox to discover the autopsy report. As I hid in the garage and bawled over reading it, the thought of her prayers being lifted up on my behalf, and the God who ordained them, sustained me. Friends and sisters and moms who just email or call or stop by: don't underestimate God's leading. Thank you for being faithful to respond!

This is tough, and tougher yet at various times or days for various odd reasons. Somewhere there is a battle going on beyond what we see here.

Nights have been hard lately. The days are becoming full and busy once again. Life is going forth out of necessity. There is noise and chaos. But nights are quiet. The mind is tired. The spirit starts to doubt and forget. The longing for my son is deep, and the dark is dark. I thank God for always waking Rob up to comfort me in the deepest parts of it.

I don't know which is worse, the crying days or the happy days. Some days I can get through the whole day and talk about Trent, look at his pictures and his belongings that are still scattered throughout the house, and smile knowing where he is. Other days I can't get through the first cup of coffee without several Kleenexes.

I still don't know how to answer the "How are you?" question. How do you sum up what God has done the past couple of months in a single reply? "Fabulous, my son is in heaven, do you want to know how to get there too? But I can't stop crying, so just go read the blog because I am a better writer than talker these days." Sometimes I can't see the happily ever after myself, how do I encourage others to?

I love my children. God has used them in an unbelievable way to minister and to teach me lately. Aren't I the one who is supposed to be leading them through this? And how do you show children how to grieve? I was pretty much just thrown in and am getting a crash course myself. I don't know what else to do except to keep pointing them to God's sovereignty, the promises of Scripture, hugging them and holding them (mostly when it's me crying), and just keep living. Each of them are individuals walking their own walk through this. Every one of them had a different relationship with Trent that I will never know the depth of. They are all grieving differently, separately, and together with Rob and I and their friends.

Their souls are my first concern, and I long for their salvation. Many a day and night I come knocking at God's door and bugging Him about it again, "Remember the other kids here, God." I have refused to make Trent's death their death. I do not want their childhood to be all about the day their brother died. They need to be allowed to live and be who God made them, as special as their brother was, and loved, adored, and cherished as much as we are loving, adoring, cherishing, and missing him. I pray for and anticipate the big plans that God has prepared in advance for each of them. The high calling that God has brought in their lives has only made them cling to Him more and seek to understand Him more. Somehow, we are just trying our hardest to keep pointing God out to them through this.

What a drab post for a drab, cold, rainy, April day. But it feels good to get it all out in writing, to somehow physically remove it from my mind and lay it at my Saviors cross that He may do with it what He wants. He said that His yoke is easy and His burden is light. I can only do one thing at a time, and if that means right now I quit trying to carry this by myself then I will gladly dump the load and just sit at my Savior's feet and worship Him again. Jesus is coming soon and His reward is with Him. Wait patiently, oh me of little faith.

Some Day

May 2, 2011

Grief never stops. Sometimes I just wish I could shut it off for a while and go have a coffee break. Go back just for a bit to what life used to be like. Other times I realize that I have just gone five minutes without thinking about Trent and then feel guilty that I should be thinking about him.

Sometimes I wonder if he really knew how much I loved him. If I remembered to tell him how much I loved him the night before the accident. Why I didn't kiss him goodbye before I left that morning. I wonder why it had to be this way. I wonder how I will go on every day missing him so badly. Why I ever took one little thing for granted. Why I ever yelled so much or insisted his school always had to be done to perfection.

Sometimes I wonder what I will do when I finally wear out all of his socks and have to buy new ones. Sometimes I can't recall his voice. Or his giggle. Or where he sat at the dinner table. Or what his favorite dessert was. Sometimes I cry myself to sleep. Nearly every night I cry myself to sleep. I don't want to enjoy life without him. Sometimes I realize this isn't just a nightmare.

Some days I want to be free from this. I don't want it to be my son who died. Sometimes I realize that just because one child died does not exempt me from any other children dying. Some days I fully trust God for that and others, well, other days I hold them closer. Some days I can't see past this world. I feel the shackles of the bondage of sin that hold me so tightly here.

I long to see heaven with my own eyes. I long for Trent. I long to hold on. To wait patiently. I long to quit crying. I long for the peace and trust again. I long to be held by my Heavenly Father who said He will wipe away every tear . . . some day.

✑ *Good Days*

May 4, 2011

I like good days. The days when I can keep it all in perspective, or, rather, the days that I draw near again to God. The days that He allows peace and joy and smiling and actually feeling emotions beyond pain. I have tried so hard to just be where God has me: the good, the bad, and the ugly. I don't like the ugly. I don't like the pain or the heartache or the despair of grief. But God leads us there sometimes. Maybe to see the depth of sin that leads to death? Maybe to hold us closer? Maybe so that on the good days we cling to Him all the more?

Today is a good day; at least it's a good morning. Only one episode of longing, close to tears, a desperate wanting of my son. I have made it a requirement that before I open my eyes and crawl out of bed I praise God and thank Him for letting Trent be in heaven. Acknowledging God's sovereignty and goodness to His children. Reminding Him and myself of the sweet verses in Scripture. Never will He leave me or forsake me; I am in the palm of my Heavenly Father's hands; God is leading me; nothing can separate me from the love of Christ, not even death; God causes all things to work for the good of His children; these present sufferings will not be worth comparing to the glory that will be revealed in us; eternity is a very, very long time and I get to enjoy it all with Trent.

> "I know that joy does not depend on circumstances; it depends on my openness to allowing Your Spirit to have control in my life. Lord, I surrender my life to You today. Make me to be known as a person of great joy."
> Author unknown.

Terri M. Stellrecht

> *You will show me the path of life; in Your presence*
> *is fullness of joy; at Your right hand are pleasures*
> *forevermore. Psalm 16:11*

Hosea 7:14

May 13, 2011

"They do not cry out to me from their hearts but
wail upon their beds." Hosea 7:14a

Lately I have been doing more wailing upon my bed than crying out to God from my heart. It hasn't gotten me anywhere, other than running away from God and losing sight of His perspective. When I can't write I know that I'm not dealing with things and only find that stuffing doesn't help either. So I write. Short, choppy, no elegance, ugly, pain, sorrow, blunt, hard. Did I say ugly already?

Right now I feel raw. Pure blood and gore and ooze. Ripped wide open raw, and it hurts to the depths of my soul. Pain with no balm other than time.

A good friend encouraged me by reminding me that missing my son is not distrusting God. So I crawl into the lap of my Heavenly Father and cry again. I go back to His Word and find strength again. And then I go back to my bed and wail upon it again. I acknowledge God who has ordained all of this, even the hurt. I praise Him that Trent is with him. Then I cry for my own pain of missing my son. For a world where there is sin. For the sorrow involved.

And then He tells me "It is okay." Okay to hurt, okay to laugh, okay to cry, okay to dance. So I go on again hurting, laughing, crying, waiting, healing, missing.

158

ℐ Wish, ℐ Wish, ℐ Wish

May 16, 2011

My brain feels fried. I feel it longing to go numb, and I fear numb more than I fear pain. I feel like I am on overdrive, stuck in four-wheel mode, working it too hard, and it's getting tougher to decipher things clearly lately. I force myself to write in the hopes of dislodging it and sorting a few things out. To lay the words on paper, or in cyberspace, to get them out of my head. To leave them here to come back to if ever need be, even if for no other reason than a way to remind myself of the fingerprints of God throughout this journey of Trent's death. To free my brain and lay my burdens down at the foot of the cross. The weight lessens with every word that is released.

I miss the first days after Trent died. I miss the absolute assurance of God's promises. The freshness of them and the great hope in them. Somewhere along the line in the past near three months the cares of this world have snuck in. My flesh and my desires have overruled. My longings have become greater than the Word of God. My heart has deceived me yet again. "Set me free from my prison, Lord, that I may praise Your name" (Psalm 142:7), I cry as the Psalmist cries. Let the praise be again from my lips, from my heart, from my whole being.

But I replace praise with wishing. Wishing that Trent would just come down those steps again this morning. Wishing that it really was his voice that I heard while I was digging in the freezer in the garage. Wishing that he could see the barn work that we dreamed about. Wishing that I could care that the garden is almost planted. Wishing that he could be the one trapping that pesky gopher in the yard instead of waiting for Rob to do it. Wishing that I could feel him in my arms again. Wishing that I would hold my other children tight, rather than being a zombie mother. Wishing that I wouldn't fight with my husband when I really just want to cry with him and have him hold me while I do. Wishing that I could be brave enough to just let the tears flow when they need to flow. Wishing that I would draw near to God again, and really trust His sovereignty and be content to patiently wait.

Out of the depths I cry to you, O Lord; O Lord, hear my voice. Let Your ears be attentive to my cry for mercy. I wait for the Lord, my soul waits, and in His Word I put my hope. My soul waits for the Lord more than watchmen wait for the morning. O Terri, put your hope in the Lord, for with the Lord is unfailing love and with Him is full redemption. God did redeem Trent from all of his sins and has only done what pleases Him and answered all my prayers for my son's salvation in doing it.

(My rendition of Psalm 130 this morning.)

Stark Raving Crazy

May 18, 2011

There is this part of grief that I am not sure if anybody has coined a term for yet. I call it stark-raving crazy. Doubt that one will make the books, but I think I should get as much of a say as anybody else who's never been in my shoes of grief before, so that's my term for it. It's the days that you want to say, "Okay God, enough, I trust you, let me wake up now." The days that you just want to go pull your son out of the closet and say, "April fools! HAHAHAHA! Fooled you all!" The days that you just want somebody to commit you to the insane asylum so you can get an IV hooked up in several different veins with lots of good drugs and go to some happy place from three months ago. Those days usually come after a couple of good days. All of a sudden it hits you after a time of total bliss and contentment and joy and smiling and wondering what in the world could you have ever been so sad about because your son is in HEAVEN after all! Then BAM! How could I be happy that my son is dead? Oh yeah, that's right God, this is the pit you were talking about when my mind takes over and my spirit forgets what Your Word says. Those guilty feelings that I was having for being happy for Your peace always bring me right back to this same miry, nasty, deep, painful pit. Throw that rope down here, will ya? I wanna go back to happy. I wanna be done now. I don't want my son to be dead anymore, God.

Here We Go

May 27, 2011

In His grace, God has brought me back again to Habakkuk. How sweet He is with His children, yet never yielding His own glory or sovereignty. How loving He is to hold us in His arms while we hurt, but then lovingly shows us a bit of His splendor when the tears have been wiped away and our hearts are ready to hear.

Of what value is an idol, since a man has carved it?
Or an image that teaches lies?
For he who makes it trusts in his own creation;
he makes idols that cannot speak.

Habakkuk 2:18

What an idol I have started to create to replace the God of the Bible. My idol doesn't take children to heaven at age twelve. My idol just might not have eternity planned out from beginning to end, including February 18, 2011. My idol just might not understand a mothers breaking heart. My idol wouldn't make their children hurt to pry their hands off of this world and turn their deceiving hearts to needing no other earthly thing, replacing it with their only need being God Himself. My idol needed to be smashed before I carved any more details into it.

Has not the Lord Almighty determined . . .
Habakkuk 2:13

Has not the Lord Almighty determined the ways of salvation? Has not the Lord Almighty determined how His glory will be revealed in the most magnanimous ways? Has not the Lord Almighty determined He would answer my prayers and make Trent dwell in heaven for eternity? Has not the Lord Almighty determined that He would prove Himself faithful beyond what I could comprehend without this? Has not the Lord Almighty determined the ways and the end and the depth of this pain and grief, only to prove Himself more faithful? Has not the Lord Almighty declared that this life is a mist, even mine? Has not the Lord Almighty used this as a wake up call for not only me, but so many others for salvation, that in eternity I will praise Him all the more?

But the righteous will live by his faith . . .
Habakkuk 2:4b

Will I live by my faith? Faith in what? My own ideas and idol of this God of the universe, or the real God who I only know through my Bible? My faith is so small. My mind so quickly forgets His promises. My heart is so easily swayed by the pain. How gracious of God to be the one who is faithful.

For the earth will be filled
with the knowledge of the glory of the Lord,
as the waters cover the sea.
Habakkuk 2:14

But the earth is not yet filled with the knowledge of the glory of the Lord. We still live in enemy territory. The deceit is everywhere, it trickles into even the believer's heart and makes us lose hope. We live short-minded and get discouraged. I forget the end. I only know how to live in the now. But one day, one day, the earth will be filled with the knowledge of the glory of the Lord. One day I will live eternally with my Savior. How I long to be found living faithfully until that day comes. How I long to be trusting and serving until it comes, rather than crying in my bed. How I long to walk it hand-in-hand with Jesus.

But the Lord is in His holy temple;
let all the earth be silent before Him.
Habakkuk 2:20

God knows what He's doing. How I pray for Him to let me trust Him in that. I try to envision Him sitting on His holy throne, His robes filling the courts, the multitude of angels and witnesses, with Jesus on His right side, with Trent before Him, face to face, knowing what I cannot imagine, seeing what I am still longing to see for myself. The Lord is in His holy temple and He does know what He's doing. One day I will too. For today I just trust.

His splendor was like the sunrise;
rays flashed from His hand,
where His power was hidden.
Habakkuk 3:4

His ways are eternal.
Habakkuk 3:6b

Splendor that I cannot even imagine. Power that I cannot even imagine. Eternity that I cannot even imagine. I bow, humbled, before this amazing God who loves even me.

> *For I am going to do something in your days*
> *that you would not believe, even if you were told . . .*
> *Habakkuk 1:5b*

How easy it is to doubt God's sovereignty. How can I believe what I cannot see? How can I believe when the waves of pain threaten to overtake? Because God said so. I hold on to my Life Preserver all the more. One day, one day, He promises to make it all right.

> *The Sovereign Lord is my strength;*
> *He makes my feet like the feet of a deer,*
> *He enables me to go on the heights.*
> *Habakkuk 3:19*

Praise Your name Lord Jesus.

I Took A Walk

June 1, 2011

I took a walk the second morning of camp. I walked up to the climbing tower where I released my son's ashes. I went alone. I just needed to be with God and cry and face it. I thought of when Trent was little and climbed that tower fearlessly for the first time. I thought of my own climb up that rock wall years ago. I thought about the joy of reaching the top and the fear and the thrill of jumping off. I thought about climbing the inside stairs three months ago. I thought about the peace and the joy. I thought about Trent's ashes flying wherever God spread them. I thought about the rest of my life without him. Then I thought about the God who said I only have to live one day at a time. Then I cried some more. I didn't fight the tears. I didn't stuff anything. I felt the pain. I let the tears flow. Just me and God facing that tower. Then I walked back the long way to chapel where a God-sent pastor was preaching a sermon about Joseph who learned to understand, just like I am learning, that God ordains all things for our good and His glory. Even the pits and the prisons and the deaths of those we love. And a friend cried with me, and laughed with me, and we had our own sermon in the midst of his. And God was there. And I did it. I faced it. I felt it. And Trent is still in heaven.

Last Night

June 8, 2011

I went to call Trent to come and eat pizza last night.

It has been nearly four months and my mind still thinks he's here. I haven't intentionally looked for him since he died. Even on the way to the hospital the night of the accident I mentally forced myself to only count four heads instead of five. But now . . .

My mind goes back and forth between wondering if he ever was here and a part of my life, like an imaginary child or something. My mind can't grasp the reality some days. It is rationalizing his absence.

But my soul knows. This mother's soul knows. The ache is because he is my son and he is not here. The joy is because he is with his Savior. The two collide. The ache and the joy cannot intermix yet. One constantly demands to rise to the top.

I have determined to not get out of bed in the mornings until I can praise God that Trent is in heaven. Some mornings I stay in bed longer, waiting for the real praise to come from my heart. Sorting this world and that world. Recalling Scripture. Remembering how good God is. Remembering that He is sovereign. Remembering how much I long to be in heaven, too.

As I lay in bed trying to fall asleep at the end of the day I look for the good works that God had prepared for me to do. I wonder how the little things that I can see could make eternal differences. I fight to live for my children who are still here. I fight to do good works for them. I pray for their salvation. I fight hiding in work to avoid feeling and grieving and loving and hurting.

I cry with my husband. Do you know how hard that is to do? To cry for your son together? He whispers God's promises to me and makes me cry again. I see God moving in him and can see some of those good works first hand before my eyes.

I long for the day this will all be made right.

Just Rambling

June 13, 2011

Suffering well is hard to do. It is especially hard when you are a people-pleaser by nature. And, I am finding, it is even harder sometimes when you are around others who have never really suffered, even other Christians. I am finding that it is a lot like raising children—everybody has their opinion on how you should be doing it. If I am not careful I find myself sinking to the expectations of those comments rather than holding on to the Promises of Scripture.

I have found that some people really don't want you to suffer well. Not on the surface, or said out loud, but maybe suffering well takes them out of their comfort zone. Maybe, somewhere deep down inside, they think that if they consider the possibility of having to suffer in their own lives they don't want to know how to do it and then God can't or won't make them suffer. Aren't we a bizarre creation?

I have been reading First Peter the last couple of days and have been so refreshed in what God is doing in my life. Peter starts out by saying that we were chosen according to the foreknowledge of God, through the sanctifying work of the Spirit, for obedience to Jesus Christ. Christ suffered for us, leaving us an example. He says that if we do suffer, we are blessed. Do not fear what they fear; do not be frightened. We are to suffer with the same attitude of Jesus because as a result we quit living for ourselves and this world and rather live for the will of God.

Peter goes on to say that one day we will give an account before God, even for how we trusted Him in suffering. We should not be surprised at the painful trials we suffer, but rather should rejoice that we participate in the sufferings of Christ, so that we may be overjoyed when His glory is revealed. So then, those who suffer according to God's will should commit themselves to their faithful Creator and continue to do good. God's mighty hand will lift us up in due time. And the God of all grace, who called me to His eternal glory in Christ, after I have suffered a little while, will Himself restore me and make me strong, firm and steadfast.

Aah! Things are put back into perspective. I can praise God for His sovereign work in my life. I can praise Him for Trent being in heaven.

What Would Trent Say?

July 13, 2011

I had the pleasure of driving Rob back and forth to work yesterday. It gave us quiet time to share what God is doing in our lives and to be an encouragement to each other, which is a very rare thing indeed to have an uninterrupted conversation twice in one day. As I was sharing some of my struggles of missing Trent he asked me, "What would Trent say to you if he could come back for just a moment?"

It made me look at things from heaven's view again, from an eternal perspective, from the side of God's sovereign plan.

What would Trent say? First of all, I can imagine the beaming smile that would be on his face. That grin from ear to ear. I can almost hear his giggle as I type this and see those sparkly eyes. He sure wouldn't want to stay for more than a moment after being in the presence of his Savior, not even for his mother. I would not want to take him from Him.

Then I can imagine him saying, "Hold on Mom, God isn't kidding! He knows what He's doing. See you when you get here! Love you!" He wouldn't encourage me to lament, or waste my time doubting, or whining, or chasing the world. He would, rather, encourage me to only live for Christ, for the gospel going out, for the complete glory of God. He would tell me to go deeper, to give up everything here, to strive to enter the Kingdom even harder, to tell others, to warn, to encourage, to strengthen.

He would share with me about God and tell me things that I couldn't even begin to imagine or comprehend. Things he could hardly start to explain in a way that I could understand them. He would make me long to be in heaven even more. He would tell me it's real, that it's worth it, to keep fighting the good fight, to keep trusting God.

I sure miss that little bugger.

Freedom!

Jesus has come to give us life and life abundantly. We have been set free. Mercy. Love. Hope. Joy. Peace. Life. Salvation. Have you ever had the overwhelming flood of God washing over you? The times when you bask in His goodness, His mercy, and His love. To feel the washing of it. The rising of joy in it. The healing and freedom found in it. The walls come tumbling down, and you let them. You know you're not worthy, but He loves you anyway. The pain and the fear have no place. Free to be who He made you in Him. When your hands are raised and there is nothing but God alone. The things you have been trying too hard to keep in check all fade away: the hurts, the worries, the cares of this world. It's all for the glory of the King. When you build walls so high and so thick sometimes you even start to wall God off. I don't want Him walled off. I want everything He promised me. I want Him. I am laying down my trowel and letting God reconstruct the ruins. I will continue to wait patiently as He does His work and will trust Him for it. Glory and praise to God forever and ever more. Amen.

Acknowledgements:

Simply writing names at the end of a book seems like an insufficient thanks to those who have accompanied me on this God-ordained journey, but it is the least I can do to acknowledge what you all have meant to me.

Where do I start? Of course, it is God that gets all the credit. This is ultimately His story. I have only attempted to write it down as He leads. To Him I owe all praise.

My husband, Rob, has been my faithful rock this side of heaven. His stubborn, firm hold to Scripture has held me firm for many years, as I could have been easily tossed by the waves of this world. His attempts at affirmation and his overwhelming encouragement for me to sit at our old computer and write have been seen and appreciated. Thanks honey! What a wonderful walk God is leading us on. Love you!

My children, Alexis, Cole, Grace and Micah, who endured fend-for-yourself-meals and a mother oftentimes unavailable because of the "other world" she was in while writing. You have all been troopers. You are my clear example of God's miracles and good works, an insight to what faith and trust really look like, and my dearest loved ones in this world. Thanks for letting Mom just sit and write in the midst of the chaos. I long to spend eternity with you, too.

Alexis, who is wise beyond my years, and who has been so clearly touched by God. Thank you for encouraging me, constantly pointing me back to Scripture, and for letting me cry on your shoulder as much as you have cried on mine. I love you my sweet girl.

To my twin sister, Traci, because I really can do anything my sister believes I can do. Because she has believed that I could write a book since we were nine years old, and here it is. Even if it's only a Christmas present for you and me, dear sister, here it is. You truly are my affirmer. XOXOXO

And of course I can't forget Uncle Jim who didn't care what I was wearing when I ministered to him and who always had such helpful advice. As long as you keep bringing me coffee pots and all those other good gifts you're worth putting up with my favorite brother-in-law. Love, #2

To my Mom, who simply loved me and longed to kiss away all of my troubles.

Thanks to my little sister, Brenda, who came just to be here with me. Who let me ramble on, who quit stuffing, who held me when I laughed and when I cried. Who allowed me to watch God work in amazing ways in her own life.

Thank you to my editor, Sarah Mattern at SheMarksinRed. com, who worked so hard to help me bring this book to completion. You are a blessing from God, Sarah!

A great big Thank You to Ryan Carlberg at WestBow Press who happily endured yet another request and revision from me.

To the friends and family that God put in our lives to physically hold up our arms as Aaron and Hur held up Moses' arms that the battle might be won. Every little thing that you did helped to carry us through the hardest days. Thank You!

To Jerry and Ashlee, the first to be here and who stayed with us through all of those hard, yet amazing, days. How do I thank you enough or acknowledge what that meant to us? To Maddie, who made me eat and sleep. To Joan, who folded my laundry too many times to count. To Bert, who believes in people living out their dreams and who taught our boys how to make long bows and cook sucker lips on a stick. To my dear friend Theresa, who kept encouraging me and giving me insight that I could not see, or maybe did not want to see.

To our First Baptist Church family who poured out their love in so many ways: Ritchard and Joyce, Jonathan and Linda, Loren and Jill, Jen, Brenda, Nels and Diane who served, Bill my teaser, Merrill who called and rejoiced with me, Sue my encourager, Bruce who was brave enough to laugh with us and kept the game going, Steve who stood amazed and Kitty who sent cards, Jason who knows my God, Blaine and Jeannie who loved us and our children, and all you other sweet souls who blessed us so much in our suffering.

And where would I be without my bloggy friends? Ladies, you do not know how special you are to me or what a big part God has ordained for you all to walk in this journey of mine~ Sherry, Cathy, RedGateFarm, Brenda, Momma Hooch, Renee, Kristen, Laura, Sonja, Janette, Teresa, Dalyn, Heather, Shoshanna, Amy, Donna, Dicky Bird, and all you other lurkers and followers. And to Anne, a long lost relative, a new-found friend.Your words and your sweet comments have brought me joy beyond measure. Thank you for being faithful dear, sweet ladies!

The list is inexhaustible. The blessings have been numerous. There are people out there that I will never know this side of heaven who have prayed for our family. Their sweet words were offered up before the throne of our King that He might receive all the glory in this through our lives. I hope I have done justice in my attempt to say "Thank You." One day God Himself will thank you all for the cups of cold water that you selflessly gave to bless us in honor of Him.

To God be the glory forever and ever. Amen.

CPSIA information can be obtained at www.ICGtesting.com
Printed in the USA
LVOW030952151111

254964LV00002B/3/P